EDISTO ISLAND:
Seaside Stories From A Geechee Gal

EDISTO ISLAND:
Seaside Stories From A Geechee Gal

Sandhi Smalls Santini

Copyright ©2020 Sandhi Smalls Santini

All rights reserved. No part of this publication may be reproduced, distributed, or transmitted in any form or by any means, including photocopying, recording, or other electronic or mechanical methods, without the prior written permission of the publisher, except in the case of brief quotations embodied in critical reviews and certain other noncommercial usage allowed by copyright law.

For permission requests, email the publisher:

sandhisantini@gmail.com
sandhisantini@yahoo.com

ISBN: 978-1-0878-9782-0
(Paperback)

Many of the historical events in this publication are factual and documented. However, any references to real people, or real places, are used fictitiously. Names, characters, and places, although factually inspired, are products of the author's imagination.

Cover photo by the author
Ancestral property, Laurel Hill,
Edisto Island, South Carolina

Dedication

In loving memory of my parents, Eugenia McKelvey Smalls (Nene), and Samuel Brantley Smalls (Bandy), whose strength, spirit, and souls are forever with me.

To my brothers, sisters, and cousins for contributing photos, lengthy conversations, and helping me connect the dots,

To my Aunt Mary E. McKelvey, the family matriarch, for clarifying certain matters,

To my big, favorite family, most precious of all, whose roots are planted deep, far, and wide,

And to my friends, and the enduring people of Edisto,

My Love and Gratitude,

Sandhi

CONTENTS

A Map of Edisto Island **9**

A Map of the South Carolina Sea Islands **10**

Edisto Island, History in Brief **11**

Edisto, The Black Republic **16**

A Committee of Freedmen On Edisto Island Reveal Their Expectations **20**

Bits-and-Pieces **23**

Routes to Roots **25**

The Smalls Family Route **27**

My Father's Side of the Family **28**

Moses Smalls **30**

Victoria Mungin Smalls **31**

The McKelvey Family Route **32**

My Mother's Side of the Family **33**

Rebecca Green McKelvey **35**

The Children of Rebecca Green McKelvey **36**

The Marriage of Eugenia McKelvey Smalls & Samuel Brantley Smalls, 1939 **37**

A Bridge To Edisto Island **38**

Growing Up Geechee On Edisto **46**

My Mother's Hats **59**

Wooden Mill Wheel From Great Grand Father Primus **60**

Wheels From Grandfather Moses **61**

A Wedding Gift From My Grandmother **62**

Grandmother Rebecca's 1905 Kerosene Lamps **65**

Uncle "SP"'s Trunk **66**

Edisto, The Isle of Churches **67**

My Mother's Church Ledgers **71**

My Mother's Handwritten Entry **72**

The Edisto Community, A Family of Families **73**

Eugenia "Nene" McKelvey Smalls, At Home In Her Kitchen **79**

Nene's Gullah Geechee Recipes:

Shrimp And Rice Pilau **80**

Sweet Potato Pone **81**

Shrimp Under Fire **82**

Chicken Liver Dip **83**

Sauteed Shrimp **84**

Mrs. Emily "MP" Hutchinson Meggett **85**

Point of Pines Plantation Slave Cabin, 1853 **89**

Miss MP's Gullah Geechee Recipes:

Lifted Up Cornbread **90**

Oyster Stew **91**

Hoppin' John **92**

Country Style Okra Gumbo **93**

Pecan Pie **94**

Home, to Edisto **95**

Samson an' Gallileah **117**

Dat Cryin' Chile **142**

References **149**

About The Author **150**

Edisto [ĕ-dĭs-tŏ] is appropriately referred to as **"Edi-Slow"**, because we Edistonians truly believe that life should be lived unhurried.

A Map of Edisto Island

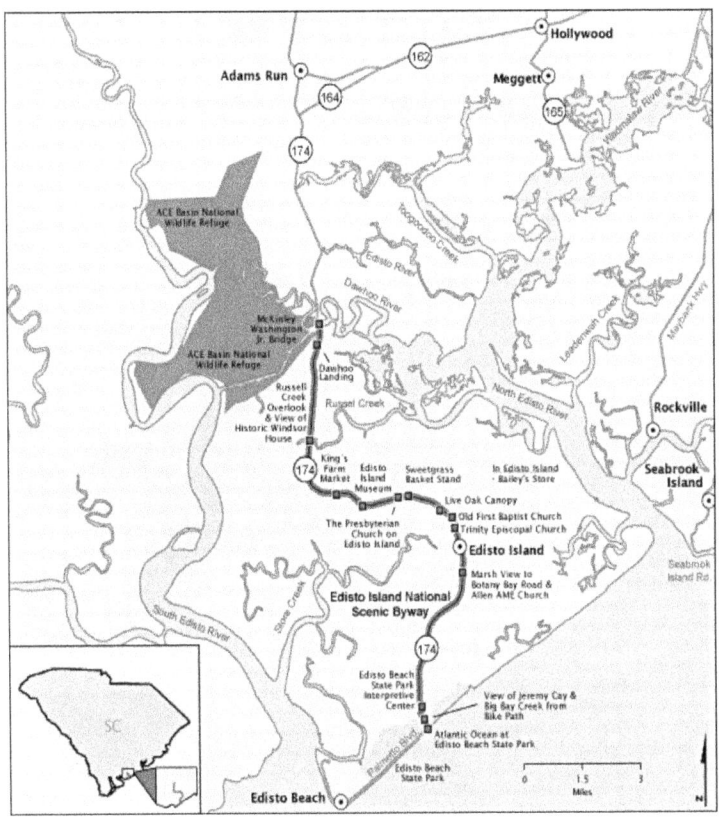

Courtesy Federal Highway Administration

A Map of the South Carolina Sea Islands

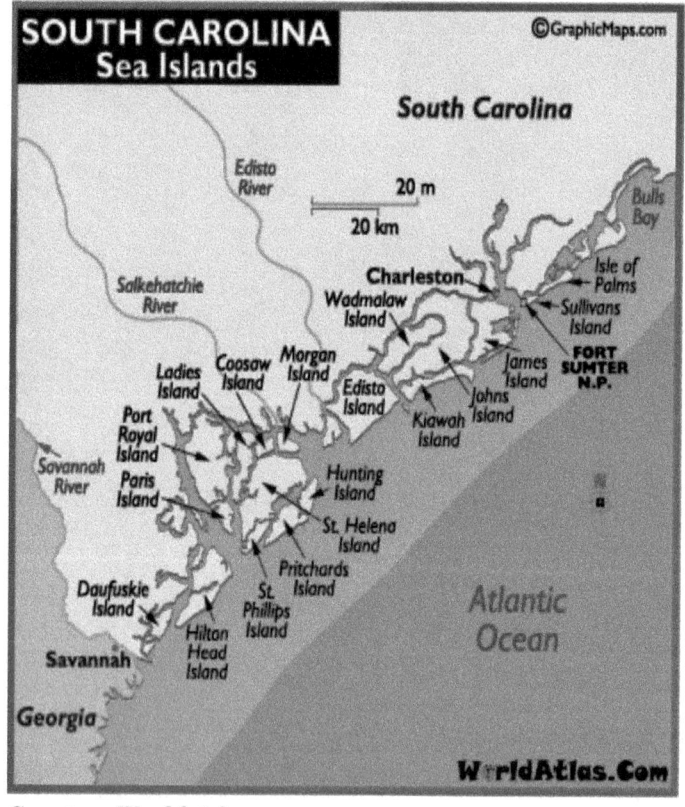

Courtesy World Atlas.com

Edisto Island History In Brief

Edisto Island is a remote barrier sea island cradled between historic Charleston and Beaufort, South Carolina. Named for the Edistow Indians, it is at once, mesmerizing and mystifying, an ancient land with a history that is as tragic as it is fascinating.

Endowed with an abundance of fruit and nut trees, camellias, cypresses, magnolias, and splendid canopies of Spanish moss-draped live oak trees, Edisto is a wilderness of wonder, ideally, and geographically, tucked away from the rest of the world. With its tidal swamps, lush, semi-tropical forests, and pristine beach, Edisto Island spans more than sixty-seven miles. It is the lowcountry, where meandering creeks, fat with oysters, clams, conch, mussels, shrimp, and crab, embrace majestically towering bluffs. Where vibrant wisterias, fragrant azaleas and gardenias flourish under ubiquitous pine and palmetto trees. And where, from nutrient-rich salt marshes, the pungent odor of "pluff mud" rises, assaulting the nostrils.

Edisto is a civilization where centuries-old cultures have communed, collided, and co-existed. First inhabited by the Edistow Indians more than 5000 years ago, these indigenous Peoples were a member of the Cusabo family of tribes. The Edistow Indians were highly-skilled hunters, fishermen, and farmers. Originally inhabitants from neighboring St. Helena Island, they settled on Edistow in the late 1500s. The island was later purchased from the Edistow Indians by the British, for mere trinkets, cloths, and tools. As a result of disease epidemics brought over by the Europeans, widespread genocide, and attacks from other tribes, by 1715, the Edistow Indians were rendered extinct.[1] As an attestation to their ancient existence, these First peoples built massive middens comprised of discarded mussel, conch, clam, oyster, turtle shells, and animal bones. More than 5000 years old, tidal creek erosion has significantly diminished the scope of the once enormous heaps of shells. Yet, remnants of these mysterious shell mounds can still be found scattered throughout Edisto Island and Edisto Beach.

During the 1600s, Edisto was colonized by the Europeans—mainly the Spaniards, the French, and the British. This was followed by The Revolutionary War in the 1700s, when British forces destroyed many of the grandiose homes on the island. Many black families were fractured and separated when slaves were captured by the British troops and sold to buyers in the Caribbean.

Eli Whitney's creation of the cotton gin in 1793 revolutionized the cotton industry in the United States and vastly increased the demand for black slave labor. South Carolina led in the advocacy of slavery, as slave labor was more in demand to work the crops. Edisto wealthy plantation owners lived a decadent life style, fueled by greed. Many of the impressive estates on Edisto were built during this time, some of which remain today.

Throughout the 17th, 18th, and most of the 19th centuries, African and Caribbean slaves on Edisto provided the life-blood that fueled the human machinery in the mass production and international exportation of purple-blue indigo, prized long-grain rice, and Sea Island cotton—once considered the world's finest. These products, all highly in demand, made white plantation owners unimaginably wealthy, and slaves, especially valuable.

In 1861, Civil War broke out. The bloodiest of all wars on American soil, it literally put brother against brother, state against state. Like Saint Helena Island, Beaufort, and Fort Sumter in Charleston, Edisto was the location of numerous Civil War encounters. At the outbreak of the Civil War, in 1860, the will of South Carolina, and its wealthy plantation owners to secede was so ardent that an Edisto slaveholder, Col. Joseph E. Jenkins, remarked in a secessionist meeting, "Gentlemen, if South Carolina does not secede from the Union, Edisto Island will."[2]

April 9, 1865 marked the beginning of the end of the Civil War. A month earlier, The Bureau of Refugees, Freedmen, and Abandoned Lands (The Freedmen's Bureau), was established by an Act of Congress to aid destitute freed black slaves and impoverished whites in the South, in the aftermath of the devastating Civil War. During the Reconstruction Era, 1863 to 1877, slavery was abolished, and remnants of the Confederacy came to an end.

The *"Forty Acres and a Mule"* initiative was a post-Civil War promise that led freed people to believe that they had a right to own the land they had once worked on as slaves. In July 1865, General William T. Sherman ordered the redistribution of lands, converting land titles into permanent deeds of ownership. Between August and October of 1865, 369 "Possessory title" certificates were issued to about ten thousand freed men and women on Edisto Island.[3]

After President Lincoln's assassination in April 1865, he was succeeded by Andrew Johnson, an old-fashioned southerner. President Andrew Johnson's Reconstruction policies, gave rise to *"Black Codes"*, which severely limited Black people's labor, income, and activities. Under Johnson, many of the possessory titles were reversed and deemed invalid. The freed people on Edisto Island were betrayed, as white plantation owners returned to reclaim their lands on Edisto. Black Codes were later replaced with "Jim Crow" laws, which continued to limit black freedoms, until the passage of the Civil Rights Act in 1964.

The last three decades of the 20th Century saw many social, political, and economic gains for African Americans on Edisto, with a huge part of its younger population leaving the once prosperous agricultural community, for more lucrative employment in and around Charleston.

Edisto
The Black Republic

In 1860, black slaves on Edisto outnumbered whites by more than four to one. The 1860 US Census reported 5082 black slaves, and 329 whites living on the island. On November 6, 1860, Abraham Lincoln, a Republican candidate, was victorious. Opposed to the election of Lincoln and his abolitionist agenda, The Secession Convention, held on December 20, 1860, voted for South Carolina to secede from the Union.

On November 7, 1861, Union troops captured Port Royal, located just outside of Beaufort. Two days later, on a Saturday, Confederate soldiers ordered that Edisto Island be evacuated of its white inhabitants. On November 9, 1861, the former slaves of Edisto Island became freed people. For them, it was, indeed, a glorious day!

One can only imagine what it must have been like on that November day in 1861, when steamboats arrived to pick up white plantation owners who were being evacuated by Union troops from Edisto. What chaos must have ensued when, with just hours' notice, slave owners and their families were forced to abandon their magnificent Antebellum mansions, and leave behind, their immense wealth, land, power, possessions, and precious cotton crops.

Plantation owners were ordered to take their slaves with them, and destroy all crops, resources, and anything of value, to prevent them from falling into Union hands. Barns, cotton houses, corn houses, and crops were burned, damaged, and destroyed. To facilitate the flight of slaveholders and their families, steamboats were sent to the ferry landing at Dawhoo Creek, at the entrance to Edisto. Barges were sent to the ferry to transport about 2000 cattle to nearby Adams Run, to feed Confederate troops encamped there.[4] White citizens fled en masse, to the mainland, abandoning the island. The word of freedom spread quickly from plantation to plantation, as slaves hid out, for days, and waited for whites to be completely removed from Edisto. The slaves who refused to leave with their owners ran away. Those who were captured were executed without a trial. Some slaves made their way by boat to nearby St. Helena Island. But most slaves remained on Edisto as freed people.

In the aftermath of the military-ordered evacuation of white inhabitants, Edisto was left abandoned by slaveholders, and without a military force in place. From November 1861 to January 1862, the freed people of Edisto, who were accustomed to taking care of their enslavers, were left to care for themselves. They had no money, and some became ill and died. But they did whatever was necessary to keep body and soul as one. Some families moved out of their drafty one-roomed shacks, into the main houses abandoned by plantation owners. They farmed the island, fished the creeks, and lived of basic provisions—potatoes, corn. Cows, pigs, and chickens were scattered throughout the plantations. Because the Geechee people viewed cotton as "the slave crop", they destroyed many cotton gins and cotton barns after slaveholders left the island.

By December, 1861, newly freed people on Edisto began setting up freedmen colonies, with refugee camps scattered throughout the island. Edisto soon became a haven for *contrabands*, escaped slaves, often arriving on the island under the protection of night. The freed people of Edisto were no longer held captive as labor by white slaveholders. Edisto became a large colony comprised of black escaped and former slaves. These are the people who would become known as the Geechees of Edisto. Among them, my maternal and paternal ancestors.

During the winter of 1861 to 1862, the black people of Edisto Island were among the first to be freed in The War Between The States. They provided for, protected, and, most importantly, governed themselves. However short-lived, for that moment, the freed people of Edisto Island lived in a "Black Republic". [5]

A Committee of Freedmen on Edisto Island Reveal Their Expectations

The following letter was written in October 1865 by a group of Freedmen from Edisto Island, South Carolina, to the Commissioner of the Bureau of Refugees, Freedmen, and Abandoned Land (The Freedmen's Bureau), during a time when freed slaves, under Union control, were allowed to cultivate the lands on Edisto that were previously owned by slaveholders.

[Edisto Island, SC. October 20 or 21, 1865]

"General It Is with painful Hearts that we the committe address you, we Have thorougholy considered the order which you wished us to Singh,1 we wish we could do so but

cannot feel our rights Safe If we do so, General we want Homesteads; we were promised Homestead's by the government,2 If It does not carry out the promises Its agents made to us, If the government Haveing concluded to befriend Its late enemies and to neglect to observe the principles of common faith between Its self and us Its allies In the war you said was over, now takes away from them all right to the soil they stand upon save such as they can get by again working for your late and thier all time ememies. If the government does so we are left In a more unpleasant condition than our former

we are at the mercy of those who are combined to prevent us from getting land enough to lay our Fathers bones upon. We Have property In Horses, cattle, carriages, & articles of furniture, but we are landless and Homeless, from the Homes we Have lived In In the past we can only do one of three things Step Into the public road or the sea or remain on them working as In former time and subject to thier will as then. We can not resist It In any way without being driven out Homeless upon the road. You will see this Is not the condition of really freemen You ask us to forgive the land owners of our Island, You only lost your right arm. In war and might forgive them.

The man who tied me to a tree & gave me 39 lashes & who stripped and flogged my mother & my sister & who will not let me stay In His empty Hut except I will do His planting & be Satisfied with His price & who combines with others to keep away land from me well knowing I would not Have any thing to do with Him If I Had land of my own. that man, I cannot well forgive. Does It look as If He Has forgiven me, seeing How He tries to keep me In a condition of Helplessness General, we cannot remain Here In such condition and If the government permits them to come back we ask It to Help us to reach land where we shall not be slaves nor compelled to work for those who would treat us as such we Have not been treacherous, we Have not for selfish motives allied to us those who suffered like us from a common enemy & then Haveing gained our purpose left our allies In thier Hands There Is no rights secured to us there Is no law likely to be made which our Hands can reach. The state will make laws that we shall not be able to Hold land even If we pay for It Landless, Homeless. Voteless. we can only pray to god & Hope for His Help, your Infuence & assistance

With consideration of esteem your Obt Servts In behalf of the people

Henry Bram

Ishmael Moultrie

yates Sampson"[6]

Bits and Pieces

The following is a collection of bits-and-pieces of my life, growing up, as a Geechee gal on Edisto Island, South Carolina. I've included herein, historical portraits of my paternal and maternal ancestors, shared moments and memories with family and friends, photos of family treasures, and a suite of tales and short stories set on Edisto Island. In short, it is a potpourri of voices, smells, sights, and sounds of bygone days. And being the proud, well-bred Geechee gal that I am, for your pleasure and partaking, I have also included, several of my extraordinary mother's prized recipes, which you will find under *"Nene's Gullah Geechee Recipes"*. As well, the indomitable

Mrs. Emily "MP" Meggett, *"The Meggett Family Matriarch, and Queen of Edisto"*, has graciously allowed me to include some of her famous mouth-watering recipes, which you will find under **"Mrs. Emily 'MP' Meggett's Gullah Geechee Recipes"**.

As you read Edisto Island: Seaside Stories From A Geechee Gal, I hope you will discover, tucked somewhere between the lines, a lesson to be learned in life.

Routes to Roots

Researching African American roots prior to the American Civil War is a daunting task, considering the status of African Americans, loss of records due to war, natural disasters, fires, the absence of accurate record-keeping and misspelled names, along with the dismaying fact that many black slaves did not have surnames. Also, as a form of punishment, slaves were often separated and sold away from their families, further fracturing bloodlines and family ties. Even tracing African American lineage post-Civil War, from the Reconstruction Era, 1865 to 1877, when the United States sought to define the legal status of African Americans, is rife with challenges.

In search of finding *routes* to my own *roots*, I have had to rely on family members and good old-fashioned word-of-mouth, precious information that has been passed down from generation to generation. However, to paint a more complete portrait of both sides of my family, I have also obtained information from *The National Archives and Records Administration, The United States Freedmen's Bureau, Federal Population Censuses, Public Death Certificates and Burials, FamilySearch.org, Ancestry.com,* and the *Federal Slave Census Schedules 1850 and 1860 (In 1850, for the first time, The United States Census listed slaveholders and included age, gender, and color of their slaves, on a separate schedule).*

The Smalls Family Route

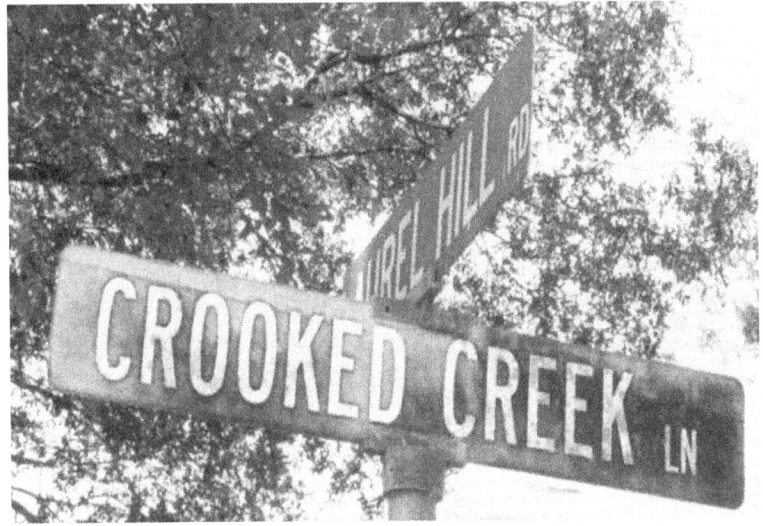

Laurel Hill Road leads to my ancestor's home site on Laurel Hill Plantation, Edisto Island

My Father's Side of the Family

My paternal great-great-grandfather, April Small(s), was born circa 1814. My great-great-grandmother, Amberta "Cumbo" Small(s) was born in 1819. The actual date of their marriage is unknown. They had one son, Primus Smalls. April and Amberta resided on Edisto Island and Saint Helena Island, South Carolina. They were both slaves.

My great-grandfather, Primus Smalls, was born in 1858. He was an only child. My great-grandmother, Amelia Golden Smalls was born in 1860. Primus and Amelia were married in 1877, and had 14 children.

They lived on Raccoon Island, and later, Laurel Hill Plantation, on Edisto Island, South Carolina.

My grandfather, Moses Smalls, was born in 1885 in Saint Helena Township, South Carolina. My grandmother, Victoria Mungin Smalls was born in 1888, in Saint Helena Township, South Carolina. They were married in 1906 and had 6 children. Moses and Victoria lived on Laurel Hill Plantation, Edisto Island, South Carolina.

My beloved father, Samuel Brantley Smalls, was born August 1, 1916, on Laurel Hill Plantation, Edisto Island, South Carolina.

Moses Smalls
August 1885 - October 21, 1959

Moses Smalls, my paternal grandfather

Victoria Mungin Smalls
January 29, 1885 -March 19, 1955

My paternal grandmother, Victoria Mungin Smalls

The McKelvey Family Route

Road in Indigo Hill, named after my maternal grandfather, Isaac McKelvey

My Mother's Side of the Family

My great-great-grandfather, Jacob Mckelvey, Sr., was born May, 1840, on Edisto Island. My great-great-grandmother, Martha Blunt McKelvey, was born February, 1837, also on Edisto Island. They were married in 1860, and had 9 children. Jacob and Martha lived in Indigo Hill, Edisto Island.

My great-grandparents, were Jacob McKelvey, Jr., and Elizabeth Eliatt (Eliott) McKelvey. Jacob, Jr., was born September, 1876 on Edisto Island. Elizabeth's birthday is unknown.

My great-grandfather, Sanders Green, was born December, 1858, in South Carolina. My great-grandmother, Dolly Reid Green, was born March,

1865, on Edisto Island. Sanders and Dolly were married in 1878.

My grandfather, Isaac McKelvey, was born in 1881, on Edisto Island. My grandmother, Rebecca Green Mckelvey, was born in July, 1887. They were married ca. 1915-1916.

My beloved mother, Eugenia McKelvey Smalls, was born January 1, 1922, on Edisto Island.

Rebecca Green McKelvey
1890 – February 28, 1943

My maternal grandmother, Rebecca Green McKelvey

The Children of Rebecca Green Mckelvey

(left to right) My uncle, Jacob Elliott McKelvey, my mother, Eugenia "Nene" Mckelvey Smalls, my aunt, Mary E. McKelvey, my aunt, Juanita Carter, my uncle, Sanders "SP" Prince McKelvey.

The Marriage of
Eugenia McKelvey Smalls and Samuel Brantley Smalls
1939

My mother, Eugenia "Nene" McKelvey Smalls, and my father, Samuel "Bandy" Brantley Smalls

A Bridge To Edisto Island

As a child, growing up on Edisto Island, I don't know how many times I'd ask my parents why was Edisto so far away from *everywhere*. At some point in my innocent mind, I had concluded that Edisto sat at the very end of the world. It had to. That would also explain why there was so much water all around, and so many green, green trees. The Creator had to stash all of that extra stuff somewhere. This was a notion that was invariably confirmed by my parents—both of whom, I'm sure, after a day of journeying to and from Charleston, left them feeling the same way I did. To this query, my mother, *Nene*, would simply reply that it only *felt* that way. While my father, *Bandy*, completely, and emphatically, agreed with me—*Edisto was at the end of the world!* After all, if you did not own a boat, and most people did not, there was only one way on and off of the island—the old Dawhoo Bridge (which is now the McKinley Washington, Jr. Bridge).

Extending over the Dawhoo River and the intracoastal waterway, the Dawhoo Bridge stood at the entrance to Edisto, connecting the island to the mainland, by way of South Carolina Highway 174. My parents remembered it as a wooden structure, a manually-operated swing bridge that opened in 1920. It was hand-cranked by an operator who watched over river traffic. Upon approaching, a vessel would sound three horn blasts, signaling the operator to allow passage. The operator would then open the bridge. By the time my siblings and I came along, the bridge had been somewhat upgraded with two lanes and limited electrical power. But it still took awhile to open, and it closed slowly. Sometimes, that old bridge refused to close. There were many times when, after ships had passed through, the swiveled bridge would not close, leaving travelers stuck on one side of the island, or the other. There were days when school children sat on buses for hours, waiting for a barge to arrive to help close the bridge. That was before cell phones came into being. Thanks to something back then called "party lines", one well-placed call to the right person, was all it took to let parents know that their children were just across the water. Unfortunately, there were also those times when people died because they were unable to get to a hospital in time.

In 1993, the Dawhoo Bridge was replaced with The McKinley Washington, Jr. Bridge, befittingly named for a beloved Edisto minister, political activist, and statesman.

I was a toddler when Reverend McKinley Washington, Jr. came to Edisto. He, and his lovely wife, Mrs. Beulah Washington, were tailor-made for Edisto. She was one of my favorite teachers at Jane Edwards Elementary School, and Reverend Washington was great for Edisto and the Sea Islands, in so many ways. When he retired in 2012, at age 75, he had served the community, and as pastor of the Edisto Presbyterian Church, for more than 50 years! Recently, I had the rare pleasure of speaking with Reverend and Mrs. Washington, by phone. Mrs. Washington's sweet voice brought back memories of some good old school days. At 83, the statesman's voice was still deep and resonant, and his mind, sharper than ever.

He was one of eight children born into a family of sharecroppers in Mayesville, South Carolina. His mother was a schoolteacher. His father did not complete elementary school. But they made sure their children received a solid education. Reverend Washington received his bachelor's degree in economics and religion, and his Master of Divinity degree from Johnson C. Smith University in Charlotte, North Carolina.

He came to Edisto in 1962, and initiated the Sea Island Comprehensive Healthcare Corporation, in conjunction with Sea Island activists and leaders, Mr. Esau Jenkins, and Reverend Willis T. Goodwin, founder of Rural Missions, Inc., a faith-based organization that serves the Sea Island communities. In 1964, Reverend Washington established the Edisto Island branch of the NAACP. During the tumultuous 1960's, he was targeted by the KKK, arrested for sit-ins, and participated in the 1963 March on Washington. When his political career took off in the early 1970's, he advocated for early childhood education, affordable housing, access to good healthcare, and the creation of local jobs for citizens. He spearheaded efforts to appropriate funds for replacing the old, problem-riddled Dawhoo Bridge.

Reverend Washington served in the South Carolina House of Representatives for 16 years, in the South Carolina Senate for 10 years, and at the Employment Security Commission for 8 years. The McKinley Washington Auditorium in the historic Avery Research Center-College of Charleston, is named in his honor.

His exemplary leadership has helped to build bridges between Edisto's past, present, and future.

With all of the island's mystique and natural attributes, most intriguing are the enduring Geechee people of Edisto Island, African and Caribbean descendants who were brought across the Atlantic Ocean on an *"unplanned trip"*. Among some of the first Africans to land on American shores, their journey is a tragedy of epic proportions, their resilient spirit, unrivaled. With feet firmly planted in the lands of Africa, and arms embracing the islands of the Caribbean, Geechees are a proud people with far-reaching roots. But it is the Geechee people's love of family, kinship, and community, that is inescapably etched deeply into their psyche. Undeterred and unshakable, their resolve to embrace and hold on to African and Caribbean ways, practices, and beliefs, definitively sets them apart from the rest of America's Afro-American populations. I should know. I was born and grew up on Edisto Island. And I am one proud Geechee gal!

Here is where I think I should define and clarify the terms *"Geechee"* and *"Gullah"*, from how I've always known both terms to be used. On Edisto Island, *"Geechee"* has always been used to define or describe us as a people. Whereas *"Gullah"* refers to the creole language that is spoken in the coastal sea islands of

South Carolina, Georgia, and Florida. Due to the broad diversity of African ethnic groups brought to the coastal sea islands, the Gullah vocabulary was created from a mixture of different African languages, and an English-based Creole. The word *"Gullah"* is perhaps, a bastardization of Angola, a republic located in Southern Africa.

In addition to rice and okra, (two of my favorite foods), the Edisto Island Geechees brought with them, African folklore and griot storytelling, tales about the supernatural, their superstitions, animal tales, religious practices, as well as root- and herbal-based medicines and natural cures. Like my parents, grand-parents, great-grand, and great-great-grand parents, I grew up heavily immersed in Geechee lore and way of life. The food, beliefs, practices and traditions, like the kitchen, backyard, and back porch stories I grew up listening to, are as much a part of me as the blood that surges through my veins. This is the backdrop of my childhood. So, it is only natural, and fitting that I should write about life on Edisto Island.

I would like to point out that there is Edisto Island, which sits in Charleston County, and Edisto Beach, located in Colleton County. Historically, Edisto Island has been, and still is, predominantly inhabited by African-American Geechees. Edisto Beach, with its summer vacation homes, and the site of our beautiful and scenic South Carolina State Park, has always been populated by whites, tourists, and visitors. As an Edistonian, I take pride in saying that both communities have always gotten along quite well. And over the years, have found it quite beneficial to live and work together, in a unified manner.

As the rest of the world continues to turn and change, I take pleasure in knowing that so much of Edisto remains protected, unchanged, and unspoiled. This is due in great part to the good people of Edisto Island and Edisto Beach, as well as to the dedication and initiatives of churches, community leaders, and organizations that continue to find ways to protect and preserve Edisto's colorfully rich and storied past. One such group is The Edisto Island Historic Preservation Society (EIHPS).

Founded in 1986 by a small group of Edistonians, the mission of The Edisto Island Historic Preservation Society (EIHPS) is to preserve the culture, natural beauty, and rich history of Edisto. In addition to operating The Edisto Island Museum, EIHPS has aligned itself with residents, landowners, and other groups and organizations, in an effort to continue to research and collect historical information, artifacts, furnishings, and other pertinent items to educate the public and inform future generations. Included in its eclectic collections are artifacts, remnants, memorabilia, literature, and information on the Edistow Indians, the island's indigenous peoples, first European settlers, enslaved African Americans, The Civil War, and the role of cotton during Edisto's plantation economy. Located at 8123 Chisolm Plantation Road, just off of Highway 174, The Edisto Island Museum is a great introduction to Edisto.

As well, the Edisto Chamber of Commerce continues to play a vital role in introducing visitors and newcomers to our beautiful community. The Chamber highlights the diverse attractions, activities, sights, and events that are unique to Edisto, while bringing local businesses to the forefront. It is a valuable resource of opportunities, connections, and information, that is essential to the overall growth and betterment of Edisto.

Growing Up Geechee On Edisto

I was born into a big, close-knit family, the ninth of eleven children from the marriage of my mother, Eugenia (Nene), and my father, Brantley (Bandy). I should state here, that Bandy fathered three other children outside of his marriage to my mother. All that matters, is that we are one family. The Edisto Island I grew up on, was a small village, a *family of families*. And thankfully, for the most part, it remains that way, even today.

Memory is something that is both selective and subjective. It is always taken from a personal and individual perspective. There are memories and moments that I cannot and do not ever wish to forget. Some that make me laugh out loud, and others, that fill my eyes with a flood of hot tears. I recall events in bits-and-pieces. What follows is a small mosaic of some of my memories, those fleeting, treasured, moments in time.

What makes my heart smile, is remembering my mother's lighthearted musings on Saturday nights, as I sat at our big kitchen table, fidgeting, while she washed, straightened, and braided my coarse hair. What makes my soul sing, is recalling the tall tales my father and uncles told, as they threaded, wove, and knotted meshed fisherman throw nets, while sitting on wooden crates, under that big oak tree in our backyard. And what still gives me goose pimples, are the old wives' tales, true, false, enhanced, or otherwise—those colorfully entertaining stories that went on throughout the evening, when neighborhood women gathered in our dining room, cutting patterns and shapes, circles and squares, that would later be meticulously hand-stitched together, carefully, and lovingly, creating yet another one-of-a-kind, masterpiece quilt.

I remember well, the times my brothers, sisters, and I gathered in the kitchen of our old house—each staking his favorite spot. That was before the fire, a fire my parents would say: *"took everything they'd worked so hard for, except our family and memories. But its okay, because, in the end, that is all that matters."* In that kitchen, we debated, well...just about *everything*. I think my parents enjoyed those times even more than we did. They loved the noise and chatter that came with having us all together at the same time. Even when our debates sometimes got a bit too heated, they managed to stay neutral. Nene knew exactly what to do to calm a rising storm. She'd gingerly place a freshly-baked cake, pie, or bread pudding, smack bang in the middle of the table! End of conversation.

There were a lot of mouths to feed in our family. Thankfully, my father, Bandy, like his father, grandfather, and great-grandfather, was a highly-skilled farmer and fisherman. Even if he didn't know it then, everything he ever farmed, was farmed *organically.* Which means, my father, who was born in 1916, was way ahead of the current food trends. My father sowed and harvested tomatoes, okra, watermelon, beans, cucumbers, peas, sweet potatoes, squash, corn, turnips, peanuts, and greens of every hue. His crops were fertilized with rich, dried, horse manure. His fields in Ravenwood, the Edisto community where we lived, and in Laurel Hill Plantation, where he grew up, were green, lush, and bountiful.

I will never forget those long, sweet days of spring and summer, when my brothers and I jumped into Bandy's old Mercury, and ventured into Laurel Hill with him. The narrow dirt road that led to where our grand- and great-grandparents once lived, was bordered on both sides with trees heavy from the weight of little yellow and red plums that were so sweet, you could smell the sugar in the air. The best treat came during watermelon season when, our father would prowl long rows of huge, vine-laden watermelons in search of the ripest and sweetest he could find. The sound made when he tapped the surface of the melon with the palm of his hand, revealed how sweet it was. The perfect watermelon found, Bandy would cut the big, juicy fruit from its vine, wipe it down,, and find a patch of clean, green grass, where he'd throw the melon to the ground, smashing it wide open. Our little hands dug feverishly into the cool, sugar-frosted sweetness.

Canning was second nature to the women of Edisto, and my mother was the queen of canning. She always kept a wall of shelves in our den, dedicated to her magnificent preserves. One of my jobs during canning season was to help Nene wash and sanitize boxes and boxes of wide-mouth, quart-size Mason Ball jars. Everyone jumped in when it came to cutting, slicing, peeling, and dicing all of the delicious things she would fill those jars with. Her big blue and white-speckled enamel pots at the ready, Nene would capture the flavor, color, taste, and texture of Bandy's wonderful harvests.

Nene canned okra and tomatoes, string beans, sour pickles, peaches, pears, and watermelon rinds. Her homemade jams, jellies, and flavored syrups, were unrivaled. Even now, I can smell those savory aromas that floated throughout the house, as jars of goodness sat steaming in tubs of boiling hot bubbles. They were some of the best foods gathered in spring and summer, foods that we enjoyed all winter long.

Nene was famous for her homemade blackberry, cherry, plum, and peach wines, none of which she ever drank, but all of which she proudly served to relatives and visitors. And our house was almost never without visiting relatives and friends. Here's where memory fails me. I don't recall which combination of brothers actually sneaked and drank from several jugs of Nene's homemade cherry wine, but I do remember everyone being taught a lesson that night.

My parents had gone to visit a sick relative, and while they were gone, several of my older brothers took advantage of that golden opportunity to indulge in some of Nene's red wine. I don't remember if it was Julius, Elliott, and Raymond, or Elliott, Raymond, and Dexter. But quite a bit of the dark red, fermented juices was consumed, which left the top part of the jugs empty. Realizing that Nene's keen eyes would notice this immediately, someone came up with the brilliant idea to fill the jugs with water. I was a little girl, but I knew our parents, and I was old enough to know that neither Nene nor Bandy would be fooled by this action. When my parents returned home, they were greeted with the intoxicating aroma of cherry wine, so strong, that the entire dining room was filled with its fragrance. It is said that parents have a sixth sense when it comes to their children. I'm certain my parents had a seventh, eighth, and ninth sense, when it came to us. Well, one good whiff was all it took. The boys were immediately summoned to the dining room, and ordered to open their mouths, as Nene and Bandy took turns sniffing mouths, while all along observing my brothers' varying states of inebriation. At first, they both struggled to keep from laughing at the sight of their boys so intoxicated, they could barely stand, let alone respond to the questions my parents leveled at them. Then, before I knew it, in one fell swoop, Bandy had whipped out his belt and lit into my brothers, one at a time. This took me by surprise, because Bandy rarely pulled out his belt. I was so shocked that I ran to my bed, and slept well into the following day.

   I recall vividly, those hot, humid Saturdays, when my sister Marie would pile us all into her pea-green Chevrolet Corvair, and take us on an outing to Edisto Beach for the day. The sandy beach shore was littered with conch, clam, and oyster shells, sand dollars, starfish, and those annoying jellyfish. They were plentiful back then.

I have fond memories of the times my sister Mary, who had moved to New York, returned home on holiday visits. She always brought with her, a footlocker filled with fashionable and trendy clothing for everyone. I laugh out loud when I think about the time Mary gave me a micro-mini, scallop-edged suede skirt, which I wore to school. That skirt got me into a whole lot of hot water with my oldest sister Elizabeth Laird, whom we all, dutifully called *"Queen Elizabeth",* based on her seat of power, and placement in the family. Upon learning that I had worn the flirty skirt to school, *Queen Elizabeth* made a special trip to my school, bringing with her, a proper, longer, replacement skirt!

Etched in my memory are the times my brother Elliott made me walk around our house multiple times, with *The Yellow Pages* on my head, because he wanted me to have perfect posture. (*The Yellow Pages were huge, heavy books, telephone directories of businesses that were printed on yellow pages).*

I'm filled with curiosity when I reflect on how my brother Isaac always had the shiniest, fastest, most hopped-up cars around. It tickles me to no end, when I think about the times my brother Raymond dragged me along on his dates to basketball, football, and homecoming games, because that was the only way my parents would allow me to attend events. (I was never allowed to go out on dates).

I will always remember that warm September morning in 1972, when my brother Dexter and I were baptized at First Baptist Church. I feared more for him getting dipped into the baptismal pool than I did for myself. I had practiced holding my breath underwater. Dexter was much taller, so I was terribly afraid that the minister would not be able to raise him from the water quickly enough. Dexter went under and came up without incident. When it was my turn, I was helped down into the cool water by my pastor and a deacon. My upper body ceremoniously dipped, water went into my nostrils, and I came up coughing profusely.

Despite stern warnings from our father to stay away from the *"special work"* he and our uncles did in the wooded area behind our house, curiosity got the best of my brother Kelvin and I. One day, we quietly followed Bandy, Uncle Jakey, and Uncle Leevee to the site of their *"special work"*. The men were talking and laughing quietly, as they made their way through the jungle-like forest, and did not notice us following them. It was very hot back there in the woods. The closer we got to them, the hotter it became, until we were both completely drenched in sweat. Little did we know that the tremendous amount of heat radiating from the corn liquor still in front of us would be more than we could bear.

I was seven years old the day my mother was being taken to the hospital to deliver her eleventh and last child. By then, I had already associated hospitals with sick people and death, and did not want my mother anywhere near one. I clung tightly to Nene, begging and pleading with her not to go to the hospital. My grip on her was so fixed, that it took my father and Uncle Jakey to pry me away. She finally calmed me with the promise of returning home with a little brother or sister. She delivered on her promise, and returned home with Eugene McKelvey, her namesake, and my baby brother. A fat, bouncing, live baby, McKelvey was far more entertaining than my stiff, life-size, walking doll.

My oldest sister's son, Eric, grew up in our house, and was always more like a younger brother than a nephew. I remember the time, his mother, *Queen Elizabeth,* decided she wanted Eric to come live with her on Short Street, in Charleston. Within a week's time of living in Charleston, and after having made numerous calls to Nene—his grandmother—Eric had made arrangements, unbeknownst to his mother, to be picked up. Early one Saturday morning, we journeyed in to Charleston, collected Eric and his possessions, and brought him back to Edisto Island, where he happily remained.

I remember the Sunday two girls from the Borough end of Edisto, innocently introduced me to my brother Scotty, and how I immediately thought he looked exactly like my oldest brother Curtis, and our father. The times Curtis sent for me after school had closed for the summer. Those summers spent in Washington, DC with him, my Aunt Mary, Aunt Juanita, and my cousins, the McKelveys', were precious.

I always enjoyed the visits from my father's son, Johnny. He was a great talker, and had a wonderful sense of humor. I remember, the time I stood in the yard of Mt. Olive Baptist Church, after a relative's funeral, and realized how much my sisters, *Queen Elizabeth* and Rhoda looked alike-just like our father.

Unforgettable are the times I spent with my cousins, the Smalls', playing softball, tag, hide-and-seek, and soaring in the swing that hung high from an oak tree on the "green", between our houses.

I embrace those sweet, summer days when I played hopscotch, jump rope, got my hair braided, and made mud cakes from the red clay and smooth white sand, with my cousins, the Mckelveys', in Indigo Hill.

Unforgettable are the memories of weddings, and family gatherings with my cousins, the Bennetts and Mungins. The summers in New York visiting Uncle

Jonathan, Uncle Robert, Aunt Helen, and my cousins, the Jenkinses'.

I think of the garlic and peppers that grew wild in Uncle Jakey and Aunt Sophie's big, beautiful yard. The old, footed black, iron pot in Aunt Lillian's backyard. I smile when I recall the times Bandy fought with his brother, Leevee, our uncle, and how they always made-up, over a shot of their own home-made corn liquor. The way Uncle Jakey closed his eyes and tilted his head to the side, before launching into yet another exciting story.

I still tremble when I recall the day I was playing in the old corn house in our backyard with my brothers, cousins, and several neighborhood kids. I climbed up on a shaky, straw basket, and as I attempted to hang the broken mirror onto the wall, the basket collapsed, and the mirror came tumbling down on me, severely cutting my left hand. My mother was at work, so my brothers ran to our neighbors. Mrs. Maggie Campbell, Mrs. Earnestine Campbell, and Mrs. Susan Meggett rushed over and took care of my wounds, cleaning and wrapping my hand, calming me while Aunt Lillian found someone to fetch Nene from her job. By the time Nene arrived, arrangements had been made to get me to the nearest hospital in Charleston. It took thirteen stitches to close that wound.

Friday, November 22, 1963. The image of my mother suddenly bursting into a flood of tears, as she stood ironing in front of our floor model television set. Mrs. Maggie Campbell, and Mrs. Susan Meggett, crying hysterically, as they ran to our house and leapt onto the front porch, screaming: *"Our president is dead! Our president is gone! They've killed our president!"* Those words, and their shattered voices, are forever etched in my mind.

I still giggle now, when I think about how my first friend, and friend forever, Joyce, and I laughed and giggled about everything. The time Joyce, my cousin Gilda, and I bought identical outfits to wear on our school trip to Washington, DC.

I laugh out loud when I'm reminded of how my mother allowed two of my 7-year-old cousins to name me, perhaps making them the youngest godmothers in history! The joy that filled me when my nephews and nieces were born.

My parents always believed that life should be balanced with a good education, religious and spiritual awareness, and a commitment to civic responsibilities. And they saw to it that we all attended college. Being affiliated with a church was essential. It didn't matter which church we went to, as long as, come Sunday morning, we found ourselves sitting on some church's pew. Community service was something we had to do, as good neighbors, and responsible citizens.

I am filled with a tremendous amount of pride, when I think of how, at the peak of The Civil Rights Movement, my mother, while president of the Parent-Teachers Association (PTA), found it necessary to board a plane, Washington, DC bound, along with other concerned citizens from Charleston County School District 23, to demand that the U. S. Department of Health, Education, and Welfare (HEW), immediately rectify the blatant inequities in educational facilities between black and white students. She was later vilified for organizing a successful, district wide boycott. She stayed her course. For her efforts, she was highly commended, and awarded the Governor's Plaque for Educational Equalities. She was also the recipient of a number of religious and civic awards. I'm amazed that she was able to do so much with a house full of children, and yet our home was always well-organized, clean, and kept in tip-top condition.

My Mother's Hats

Some of my mother's hats that I still wear

Wooden Mill Wheel from great-grandfather Primus

Courtesy, my brother, Eugene Mckelvey Smalls

Seed Drill Wheels From Grandfather Moses

Courtesy, my brother, Eugene Mckelvey Smalls
Wheels from a Seed Drill

A Wedding Gift From My Grandmother

A couple of months before we were married, one of my uncles, Reverend Sanders Prince "SP" McKelvey, insisted that my husband, Giancarlo and I meet with him at his home in New Rochelle, for premarital counseling. When the day came, we packed a four-course Italian meal from our restaurant, Chelsea Place, complete with wine, and brought it with us. My brother Elliott accompanied us, on what turned out to be an amazing day filled with wonderful stories and interesting pieces of information from my uncle, who was an ardent storyteller.

We were half-way through our counseling session when my eyes fell in love with two vintage lamps that sat on the top shelf of a cabinet bookcase in my uncle's study. I did not know then that they were his mother's lamps, my grandmother's lamps. I'd never seen them before, because for years, they had been hidden behind stacks and stacks of books. Uncle SP explained that the original glass shades had long ago been broken. That didn't matter to me. They were beautiful. My brother and I cleaned those lamps and placed them on the table. While eating, we talked about places where I might find replacement glass shades for the lamps, and how they could be re-purposed with small LED lights inside. I was drawn to those lamps like a moth to a flame. At the end of the day, as we were leaving, my uncle called me into the kitchen, where he handed me an envelope. He had already placed one of the lamps in a brown paper bag and was digging into a cabinet in search of another paper bag.

"Your wedding gift is in the envelope. And I want you to have these lamps". He chuckled.

"You know what's funny?", he asked, laughing, as he held the bag opened for me to place the lamp inside.

I smiled and waited for "Uncle SP" to ease into yet another one of his wonderful stories.

"I awoke early this morning to do some tidying up and something kept telling me to bring those lamps out from behind my books. It was as if someone was trying to tell me something. Now I know why."

I slid the lamp into the bag, then handed the envelope back to my uncle. After a little back-and-forth with the envelope, he finally gave in, albeit, reluctantly. It didn't matter how much money the envelope contained. As far as I was concerned, my grandmother's lamps were priceless.

1905 Kerosene Lamps, Grandmother Rebecca

A pair of lamps that belonged to grandmother Rebecca

Uncle SP's Trunk

Uncle "SP" Sanders Prince McKelvey's old wooden trunk, ca. 1940

Edisto
The Isle
of Churches

There has never been a shortage of churches on Edisto. From the island to the beach, houses of worship, of practically every denomination, are scattered across this well-preserved community. If Charleston is *"The Holy City"*, then, Edisto must surely be *"The Isle of Churches"*. Edisto is home to at least 16 churches, which includes four historic churches: *Presbyterian Church Edisto Island, New First Missionary Baptist Church, Trinity Episcopal Church, and Zion Reformed Episcopal Church.*

The churches of Edisto have traditional cruciform layouts that resemble the shape of the cross, when viewed from above. Prior to the Civil War, slaves attended the churches of their owners. Whites, exclusively, occupied the nave, or main area of the church, which was closer to the pulpit. Slaves were confined to the upstairs gallery.

What was originally Edisto Baptist Church (now New First Missionary Baptist Church), is the oldest black congregation on Edisto Island. Established in 1818 by Hephzibah Jenkins Townsend, the wife of a prominent sea island cotton planter, this was the first Baptist church on the island. After whites were evacuated from Edisto during the Civil War, the black congregation remained in the church.

My maternal and paternal great-grandparents were members of Edisto Baptist Church. My grandmother, Amelia Smalls is interred in the church's more than 200 year-old cemetery. My grandfather, Isaac Mckelvey, a carpenter and artisan, while a member of the church, painted its signature blue and white cloud ceiling. My mother, Eugenia, served as missionary and church clerk for nearly 40 years. The congregation now occupies a new building, that sits next to the original church, where my siblings and I were baptized, and several of us were married in the church. My father, Brantley, was a member of Mount Olive Baptist Church in the Borough, which was called "Little Baptist Church".

My memory takes me back to Reverend William M. Grant, who pastored the church from 1957 to 1972; Reverend Tony L. Daise, Jr., who pastored from 1973 to 1998, and Reverend Albert "Chick" Morrison, Jr., the current pastor of New First Missionary Baptist Church. Reverend Morrison was born and reared on Edisto Island. He received his early childhood education on Edisto and Yonges Islands. His religious education was obtained from Cummings Theological Seminary in Summerville, South Carolina, and Morris College School of Religious Studies, in Sumter, South Carolina. Reverend Morrison was licensed in 1992, and assumed pastorship of New First Missionary Baptist Church in 1998. As a spiritual and civic leader, his dedication to church and the Edisto community at-large, has been steadfast, as he continues to serve both with the utmost of dignity, honor, and distinction. The widowed father of two sons, Reverend Morrison has served as past president of the Edisto Island Community Association, and the Edisto Island Ministerial Alliance. He currently serves on the Board of the Rural Mission on Johns Island, and is a member of the Edisto Island Land Trust, Safe and Orderly School Board, as well as the Sea Island Cultural Arts Festival. He continues to be a role model on Edisto and beyond. In a recent conversation with him, during the 2020 COVID-19 pandemic, Reverend Morrison said:

"Love and respect goes both ways. Treat me the way I treat you. The church and I have been good to each other".

New First Missionary Baptist Church was added to the National Register of Historic Places in 1982.

Other Edisto churches include: *Allen A.M.E. Church, Bethlehem RMUE Church, Calvary A.M.E. Church, Church of Christ, Edisto Island, Edisto Beach Baptist Church, Edisto Island United Methodist Church, Edisto Presbyterian Church, Episcopal Church on Edisto, Greater Bethel A.M.E. Church, Greater Galilee Church Of Our Lord, Mount Olive Baptist Church, St. Frederick and Stephen Catholic Church.*

My Mother's Ledgers

My mother's clerical ledgers from First Baptist Church, Edisto Island, SC, 1970-72.

My Mother's Handwritten Entry

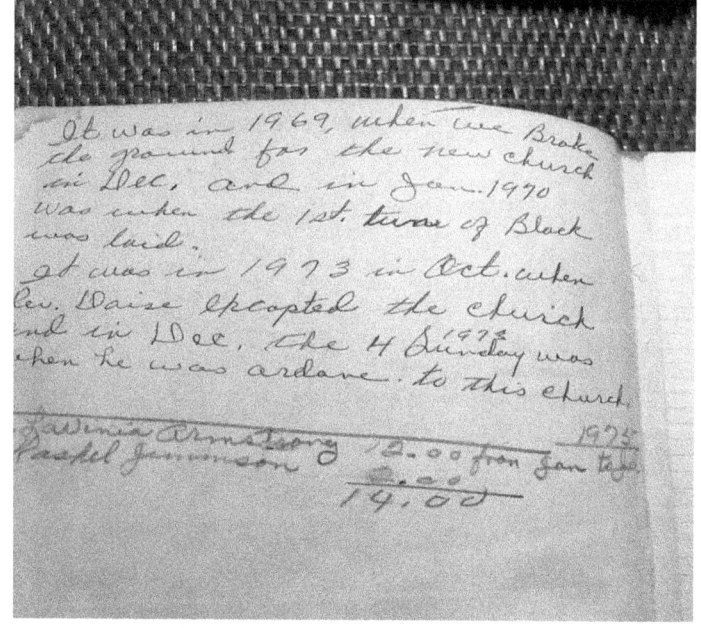

An entry referencing the 1969 groundbreaking for The New First Baptist Church, Edisto Island, SC.

The Edisto Community
A Family
of Families

Growing up, Edisto Island did not have a fire department. People simply followed the smoke, and everyone knew where to run with buckets of water and wet blankets. No cafes, fast-food stops, or restaurants. Edisto Island had some of the world's best cooks! Besides, everyone on the island hunted, fished, and farmed. And there were no shopping centers. People made-do with what they had. One thing was certain, whatever shortcomings there might have been on Edisto Island, there was never a shortage of good, home-grown foods, fresh seafood, visiting company (invited, uninvited, or otherwise), churches, or colorful, captivating stories—all of which I reveled in.

We've never had a hospital on the island. There wasn't even a clinic. As a child, the only thing that was even remotely close to a clinic was the "sick room" at Jane Edwards Elementary School. The "sick room" was a narrow, dimly-lit alcove located midway of the school's main hallway. It was furnished with one twin bed, a desk, two wooden chairs, and a tall metal medicine cabinet. And a group of loving, caring teachers took temperatures, and cleansed and bandaged cuts, scrapes, and bruises.

Jane Edwards Elementary School was the black elementary school on the island. It was named after an African-American woman who was born in 1860 in Charleston, South Carolina, and came to Edisto at an early age. She received her teaching license from Avery Institute in 1877. "Miss Jane", as she was known, taught at Central School, which was located near Steamboat Landing Road, for over 15 years, before moving on to the Borough School, where she taught for more than fifty years. She retired in 1945, after 66 years of teaching. When the new, more centrally-located, 11-room school was built in 1954, it was appropriately named in honor of the veteran teacher. "Miss Jane Edwards" was 103 years old when she died on December 16, 1963.

There were no doctors on Edisto Island. But there were *granny midwives, baby catchers, women healers, seers,* and *root workers*. A class of highly respected, reliable, well-trained, experienced women, these social workers went above and beyond the call of duty. As in the Afro-Caribbean folk tradition, they were integral to family life and overall well-being. On Edisto Island, many of them were believed to possess supernatural, healing, and magical powers. They served essential cultural, political, and socio-economic functions, and they were revered.

If my memory serves me well, I do recall that from time-to-time, there might have been a doctor on Edisto Beach. But he did not live there year-round. Like so many Edisto Beach residents, who were white, and mostly affluent, he and his family took up temporary residency during the summer months, in a vacation house on the beach.

Sometime in the early 1970s, a retired doctor from South Africa, visited Edisto while on vacation. He fell in love with the Geechees and the island, and established a practice. I don't know how he managed financially. Because, in retrospect, I now believe that he had a pro bono practice. And judging by the way Edistonians (especially teachers and preachers on the island) took to him, I suppose that had a lot to do with the doctor's incredible popularity. He had great bedside manners and a wonderful sense of humor. My parents liked and trusted Dr. Elliott. He was my doctor. Back then, *"apartheid"* and "South Africa" were words that had only recently been introduced into my young and naive vocabulary.

I looked forward to my checkups and appointments with Dr. Elliott. During those sessions, I bombarded the good doctor with questions on the issue of race relations, and waited eagerly as he thoughtfully removed thick-rimmed eyeglasses from his sun-leathered face, and searched his desk for tissue to clean the lenses. He was never too busy to answer my questions, nor did he ever appear to be uncomfortable telling me what it was like being a white South African who had once lived under the apartheid system, in a world where segregation and discrimination, based on race and color, were legal. Our appointments usually ended with Dr. Elliott recommending certain books that he thought I might enjoy reading.

Edisto Island Geechees have survived enslavement, wars, epidemics, catastrophic natural disasters, and dehumanization. Our endurance is a testament to the strength, will, and determination to survive and to hold on to our culture, our beliefs, our ways, our future, and especially our *food*.

Gullah Geechee Cuisine

My siblings and I loved our parents infinitely. We worshiped, *feared*, and adored Nene and Bandy. And we *liked* them a lot. Bandy wove flawlessly perfect fishing nets. Nene attended a Teaching Institute for black teachers in Charleston, where she actually *learned Latin!* She was a natural artist who made beautiful ceramics, arts-and-crafts, and magnificent, hand-sewn patchwork quilts. They were salt-of-the-earth people- goodhearted, decent folks who made the most out of what they had, and gave generously. They found in each of us, a special quality, and taught us the importance of giving and sharing, especially when it came to food.

There were a lot of mouths to feed in our family. Somehow, our parents always made sure there was enough food for us, with extra space and food at the table for company, relatives, and friends. And there were always guests. The smell of Bandy's savory oyster stew with bacon, onions, and hot red peppers, and his piquant catfish stew, still entice my nostrils. Back then, it was common to eat turtle eggs. I was told that my grandmothers even used turtle eggs to bake cakes. Bandy's spicy turtle soup would burn a cold or flu right out of your body. We no longer eat them. Now, we're protecting them from extinction. *(The Loggerhead sea turtle is South Carolina's state reptile. Since 1978, it has been listed as "threatened" on the United States Fish and Wildlife Service Endangered Species List).*

Like the culture, Gullah Geechee Cuisine is rich, colorful, and unique. The dishes are full-flavored, appetizing, and savory. There's always rice and seafood somewhere on the table. Sweet potatoes, okra, tomatoes, corn, beans, peas, peanuts, watermelon, peppers, grits, and greens of every hue, are staples. The Gullah Geechee cuisine is known for its palatable "one pot" meals such as *Hoppin' John, Okra Gumbo,* and *Rice Pilau.* In keeping with tradition, the foods and the way food is prepared can be traced directly back to our African-Caribbean roots. Gullah Geechee dishes were made mostly from fresh caught seafood, cured meats, and freshly picked farmed vegetables, fruits, and berries. On Edisto, fresh seafood was always in abundance. The creeks were ripe with oysters, clams, crab, conch, shrimp, mullets, porgies, catfish, flounder and sea bass. Venison and other wild game were seasonal and plentiful. Pork was almost always smoked and cured.

Nene loved cooking, and she was extraordinary in the kitchen. For many years she managed the cafeteria at Baptist Hill High School on Yonges Island, South

Carolina. But what delighted her even more than cooking, was seeing others enjoy her delicious dishes.

Here are some of *Nene's Gullah Geechee Recipes*

Eugenia "Nene" McKelvey Smalls,
At Home In Her Kitchen

My mother, Eugenia, making Sweet Potato Pone in her kitchen, during a Charleston Post and Courier interview

Nene's Gullah Geechee Recipe

Shrimp And Rice Pilau
Yields 6 Servings

3 cups rice
3 pounds medium, boiled shrimp
1 medium onion
Salt, pepper, and sage to taste

Cook rice, preferably in a steamer. Clean and boil shrimp, then fry in butter or fat until glossy. Add minced onion, salt, pepper and sage. When browned, add shrimp, onion, and seasonings to rice. Let simmer for 5 minutes to allow rice to absorb shrimp flavor.

Nene's Gullah Geechee Recipe

Sweet Potato Pone
Yields 24 slices

3 quarts, orange yams, preferably fresh, grated
½ pound butter
2 cups sugar
Dash of ground nutmeg
Juice and grated hull of 1 large orange
1 tablespoon lemon juice

Combine ingredients in a heavy cauldron. Cook uncovered on low heat for 1 hour. Stir occasionally to avoid scorching mixture. When yams turn brown, pour mixture into greased baking dish. Smooth top of mixture with spoon back. Bake for 1o minutes at 350 degree oven until top is slightly crusty. Serve hot, room temperature or cold.

Nene's Gullah Geechee Recipe

Shrimp Under Fire

- 2 lbs. Large unshelled shrimp
- ½ cup Bacardi dark Rum
- ½ stick butter, melted
- ¼ cup minced parsley
- 1 lb. Lemons, juiced
- 2 crushed garlic cloves
- 1 teaspoon salt
- ¼ teaspoon freshly ground pepper
- 2 tablespoons Bacardi dark Rum

Leave tail on shrimp. Peel, devein, and rinse well. Cut slightly through, lengthwise, and flatten. Combine remaining ingredients with exception of 2 tablespoons of rum. Place mixture in frying pan. Heat. Add shrimp and coat well. Cook over low heat until shrimp turns pink. Splash 2 tablespoons of rum evenly over shrimp.

Nene's Gullah Geechee Recipe

Chicken Liver Dip
Yields about 1 1/3 cups

½ lb. Chicken livers cut into small pieces
2 lbs. Butter, melted
1 clove, pressed or minced garlic

Sautee livers till cooked through.
Stir in:

3 tablespoons Bacardi dark Rum

Let cool. Combine mixture in a blender with:

1 pckg. 8 oz. Softened cream cheese
¼ cup plain yogurt
½ teaspoon salt
¼ teaspoon crushed dried or fresh basil

Salt and pepper to taste. Blend well until smooth. Serve with crackers or raw vegetables.

Nene's Gullah Geechee Recipe

Sauteed Shrimp

1 ½   lbs. Medium shrimp, shelled, deveined, cleaned thoroughly
½   cup Bacardi Light Rum

Marinate for at least 4 hours.
¼   cup butter

Melt in large, heavy frying pan. Add shrimp and rum mixture with:
½   teaspoon garlic salt or crushed garlic
Sautee 8 to 10 minutes until shrimp is cooked throughout. Sprinkle 1/3 cup grated Parmesan cheese and freshly ground pepper over shrimp. Broil briefly until cheese is slightly brown.

Mrs. Emily "MP" Hutchinson Meggett
Preparing a Gullah Geechee Dish

Mrs. Emily "MP" Meggett, family matriarch and "Queen of Edisto Island".

Mrs. Emily Hutchinson Meggett's roots are well-planted in the soil of Edisto Island. "Miss MP", as she is affectionately called, is known as the "Queen of Edisto Island"--a crown and title which she has rightfully earned. At 87 years young, the Meggett family matriarch has given more of herself than most people will give in two lifetimes. Renowned for her mouthwatering Gullah Geechee dishes, Miss MP's generosity and constant acts of selflessness, are unrivaled. She is a woman whom I have loved and adored my entire life. We speak often. I enjoy our conversations, and I always learn something new from her. Miss MP frequently declares that "Edisto is the most blessed place on earth". I happen to agree with her. After all, who am I to disagree with The Queen of Edisto Island?

The mother of ten children, Mrs. Meggett has cared for, nurtured, and fed, practically everyone on Edisto Island *and* Edisto Beach, at one time or another. Her faith in God, and devotion to community, are unwavering. Her family has lived on Edisto Island for generations, and can be traced back to pre-Civil War times. She was one of the first members to be baptized in the new pool at First Baptist Church, (now New First Missionary Baptist Church). The pool has since been covered up. Mrs. Meggett took over as church clerk after my mother retired from that position. For years, she prepared home-cooked meals and personally delivered them to Edisto's sick and shut in. Miss MP has graciously allowed me to include here, some of her famous, delectable, Gullah Geechee dishes, which you will find under **Miss MP's Gullah Geechee Recipes.**

Mrs. Emily Meggett is the widow of Mr. Jesse Meggett, who was born and grew up in the historical

Point of Pines Plantation Slave Cabin on Edisto Island. A living testament to the endurance of a family, the 1853 slave cabin, donated by the Edisto Island Historic Preservation Society, is now a main attraction of the Smithsonian's National Museum of African American History and Culture (NMAAHC), in Washington, DC. The slave cabin was listed in the National Register on November, 28, 1986. One of two remaining slave dwellings left on Edisto Island, the Point of Pines Plantation Slave Cabin was highlighted in the museum's inaugural exhibition, *"Slavery and Freedom"*.

Built on Charles Bailey's Point of Pines Plantation in 1853, the dwelling was one of nine other similar cabins that were built in a row. A two-room dwelling with one door and three windows, the structure was made of Southern yellow pine, lath, and cypress. It measured 73" H x 246" W x 186" D., had a timber frame, kerosene lamps, and a pot-bellied wood burning stove. The childhood home of Miss MP's late husband, Mr. Jesse Meggett, the cabin was inhabited by family members until 1981. At the Point of Pines Plantation, there were 75 black slaves who lived in such cabins before and after Emancipation.

Point of Pines Plantation Slave Cabin, 1853 Edisto Island, South Carolina

"Slavery and Freedom" exhibition, The National Museum of African American History and Culture, Washington, DC (Gift of The Edisto Island Historic Preservation Society)

Miss MP's Gullah Geechee Recipe

Lifted Up Cornbread

- 2 eggs
- 2 heaping tablespoons Crisco (or oil)
- ½ cup sugar
- ½ cup flour
- 1 ½ cups cornmeal
- 1 teaspoon lemon extract
- 2 cups milk (if too stiff, add more milk)

Mix all ingredients. Bake in 350 degree oven for 20 to 25 minutes, until golden brown. You can add walnuts, pecans, raisins, or more sugar, if desired.

Miss MP's Gullah Geechee Recipe

Oyster Stew

½   stick butter
½   cup celery
Cook in double boiler 20 minutes. Add:
1   cup milk
1   pint half and half
    pinch of salt
¼   teaspoon Accent
When hot, add:
1   pint oysters with juice

Remove from heat. Set over double boiler for 3 to 5 minutes. Add 4 to 5 shakes of Worcestershire sauce. Add 6 to 8 saltine crackers, crumbled. Serve immediately.

Miss MP's Gullah Geechee Recipe

Hoppin' John

1\. large onion, cut up or grated
2 cups dry field peas (cow peas)
2 slices salted butts meat
2 ham hocks
2 ½ quarts of water

Cook down until peas are done. Remove meat. Add:

2 cups of rice

Stir with wooden fork until all water is absorbed. Then put in steamer. Steam until done.

Miss MP's Gullah Geechee Recipe

Country Style Okra Gumbo

2 ½ tablespoons oil
1 package okra
1 large onion
1 green pepper

Heat oil in large skillet or pot. Add okra, onion and pepper. Fry for 5 minutes. Add:

1 quart can tomato with 1 ½ cups of water (or 1 can tomato paste with 3 ½ cups water).

1 tablespoon sugar

Turn to lowest heat, when mixture comes to a boil. Let simmer for 1 ½ hours. Season with salt, Accent, seasoning salt, and 1 tablespoon thyme leaves. Add pieces of ham or shrimp. Serve with rice.

Miss MP's Gullah Geechee Recipe

Pecan Pie

Add to mixing bowl:

- 3 eggs
- 1 cup brown sugar
- 1 cup Blue Label Karo
- 2 tablespoons butter
- 1 teaspoon vanilla

Beat until firm. Have crust ready.
1   cup pecans cut up.

Add pecans to uncooked crust. Pour mixture over pecans. Bake in 350 degree oven for 45 minutes. Remove from oven immediately. It will congeal when it cools.

Home
To Edisto

On this early Saturday morning, the busy Port of Charleston was teeming with excitement. Farmers, fishermen, and hunters from nearby St. Helena Island, St. Johns Island, Wadmalaw, Beaufort, and Edisto Island, had arrived long before day-clean to set up shop. As always, the cobblestone streets were overcrowded with merchants and shoppers eagerly eyeing the best possible deals and prices on lumber, poultry, animal skins, furs, tobacco, indigo, cotton and rice. The noisy Dock Street Market was surpassed only by the masses who had ventured out to welcome the return of *The Royal Magnolia,* an English steamboat unmatched in size and beauty.

Zebedee made his way through the bustling crowds, stopping occasionally to chat with some of the men he had become acquainted with. Others were familiar but nameless faces. To them, he simply nodded. He stopped for a moment to mop the sweat from his forehead with the back of his hand. It would be a long, tiring day. But then, so were all of his days.

Zebedee McKelvey was a stately man with well-defined features. His thick, wavy hair stood at least two inches on his head. His eyes, dark, deep, and solemn, had seen so much more than his twenty years of life. "Zeb", as everyone called him, rarely smiled. But when he did, it came from a place deep down inside of him. Smart and well-spoken, with an imposing stature, he was strong and gentle, at the same time, something that made everyone feel comfortable in his presence. In short, there was nothing about Zeb that anyone could not like. Even if some men were just a bit jealous, they still respected him. His birth, however, on a stormy summer night, was one that the folks on Edisto Island would never forget.

Now, the way the old folks tell it, his was either a *"blessed"* or *"cuss"* birth. But as far as his Aunt Virtue was concerned, she had no doubt that Zeb was a blessing to this world. The way Aunt Virtue saw it, her nephew Zeb, whom she loved more than life itself, was just in a hurry to be born. And, he was just possibly born in the wrong place, at the wrong time. No one knew for sure why, but, everyone in the house that night who witnessed Aunt Virtue ketching that long baby from her dying sister, agreed that Zebedee Cyrus McKelvey bolted into this world.

Miss Dolly was a little, strong lady. She was always willing to help out when it came time to birthing babies. She knew exactly what to do *before* the baby came, *while* it was trying to be born, and *after* it was born. She had come prepared to help Aunt Virtue as much as possible, and to stay for a few days, if need be. For Virtue and her husband Sanders, she brought a big pan of fried fish, red tomato rice, sweet corn, biscuits, and a blackberry pie. Big Hebba, on the other hand, had a reputation for always coming around just in time for supper, which was exactly what she had done on that night. While Big Hebba was enjoying Miss Dolly's wonderful meal, outside, a wicked storm was brewing. Between the wind, rain, and flying branches, Aunt Virtue, Sanders, and Miss Dolly talked Big Hebba into staying the night. They thought it was too dangerous for her to try to make it back to the Seaside in her mule and wagon in such evil weather. Besides, Miss Dolly told her that they'd be up all night long anyhow, waiting to ketch Alvira's baby, and they could use some extra hands.

Aunt Virtue sat on a wooden crate that was jammed between the bed and the wall. It was covered with a piece of clean cotton fabric. At the foot of the bed was a small stool, where, when the time was right, she would sit to ketch the newborn. She held on to Alvira's hand, and wiped sweat away from her forehead, with the other. For the past several days, she had seen her younger sister wasting away. Sick with fever, talking out of her head, and unable to keep food down. There were signs that Virtue and Miss Dolly had seen before. They would hope for the best, but had already prepared themselves for the worst. Shortly after midnight, they heard a ferocious roar of thunder. A flash of blue lit up the night, and lightning struck a tree, sending a heavy branch crashing to the ground. As her life ebbed away, Alvira let out a long, piercing scream, then took her last breath.

Like the storm raging outside, the baby bolted out screaming and kicking, with arms flailing in every direction. Aunt Virtue, grabbed the child, cut his cord, then handed him over to Miss Dolly. Realizing that her sister was gone, and wracked with grief, she quickly cleaned herself up and went to her sister's bedside, where she took her still warm hand, knelt down and prayed, sorrowfully.

Before Big Hebba and Miss Dolly could wash the child, his bright eyes had sprung wide open, and stared up at the two women as if he'd known them. It was when Big Hebba saw four teeth in his mouth, two above, and two below, that she started hollering at the top of her voice. She screamed so loud, that the poor frightened baby hauled off and bit her. They said it was some sight, seeing Big Hebba drop that baby right into Miss Dolly's lap, then ran around the table shouting, chanting, and *"speaking in tongues"*. It was something they would never forget. And even now, folks still talk about it.

Three years after Zeb was born, a young lady with a shy little boy in tow, came to visit Aunt Virtue. She had traveled from Wadmalaw Island in a dugout canoe with the child, and had come to tell Aunt Virtue that he was three years old, and the son of her older brother, Marcellus. Virtue took one look at the boy and saw every bit of her brother in the child's face. She let out a little laugh. His forehead, eyes, nose and mouth, were all Marcellus'. Virtue hadn't seen her brother in years. He was a seaman who worked mostly on cargo ships that sailed between Charleston, the West Indies, and Europe. Between Charleston and Wadmalaw Island was where he usually stayed on his short returns to America.

"Him name Marcellus, same like e fatta", the girl mumbled.

"Born Christmas day tree yays 'go".

The young lady left a bag of clothes for the boy, and a small brass locket with a photo of her and his father. She handed Aunt Virtue some coins, and promptly left. She was never heard from, nor seen of again. Aunt

Virtue and Marcellus took well to each other. But nothing delighted him more than when Aunt Virtue took him to the back of the house and pulled back a curtain, where, in a small bed, Zeb laid sleeping. The cousins grew up as close as brothers.

Spring had come early this year, and from the look of things, so would summer. It was the first week of March, but already the azaleas and jasmines were primping with pretty flowers. The Angel Oaks, cypresses, and magnolias stood majestically, waiting to offer shade on hot summer days that would surely come. Zeb took in the air, sweet with the fragrance of pine and palmetto. Every now and then, a soft breeze made its way across the harbor. Zeb drew in a long, deep breath. For a moment he felt himself drifting away from the sounds and smells on the dock. His mind drifted, and followed his heart across the water and marshes...to a road of red clay, where trees, heavy with sugary sweet plums, hung over the ground, covered with purple juice from blackberries. He missed Aunt Virtue and Marcellus. And he was homesick for Edisto. He had taken on the job of valet and footman for Mister Huntington because it was steady work and paid well. I helped that Mister Huntington was a decent and honorable man. Zeb needed the money to help Aunt Virtue meet her tenancy and sharecropping obligations on Edisto. She and Marcellus farmed as much as they could, but they could never make enough money to share profits with the landowner, *and* still have something left over for them to live on. Working for Mister Huntington meant living in Charleston half of the year, during the winter, and spending the spring and summer months working for him at their summer home at The Bay on Edingsville Beach on Edisto. The Huntingtons were always entertaining guests from abroad. Visitors and relatives arrived all summer long from Barbados and Europe. There were parties and dinners practically every night. He still had to put in his hours of work, and sometimes he worked even harder with the out-of-town guests who ordered him around. But at least he was on Edisto and that meant he could spend his one day off, visiting with Aunt Virtue and Marcellus. A few more weeks, and he would be heading to Edingsville Beach, a stone's throw away from the house on Edisto where he was born.

"Zeb!", shouted a familiar voice. "Over here!"

Zeb's eyes searched the busy marketplace for his cousin Marcellus. They were only a few feet away from each other when their eyes connected. Zeb, who stood at least a foot over Marcellus, extended his long leg over a pile of bags on the ground and leapt over to them to greet his cousin. Marcellus smiled, stood back, and looked up at Zeb.

"Boy, aint ya' neva gon' stop growin'?", he teased.

"An' I see you done stop growin", Zeb shot back. They grinned and hugged, more like two little boys than young men. They both let out laughs that were almost identical. Despite the difference in their heights, their mannerisms and personalities were quite similar. And they certainly looked a lot alike. Most people would have thought they were brothers.

Zeb waved at some of the other men from Edisto. The day was just starting and already they looked tired. They were unshaven, with red eyes and tobacco-stained teeth. Their rumpled clothing told Zeb that they had spent the night, outside on the dock. None of that mattered. He was happy to see them, and they were happy to see him. They were from Edisto, and that made them all family.

"How Aunt Virtue and Uncle Sanders faring?", Zeb asked, leaning to one side to get a good look at his cousin's face.

"Dey is good. Ya' know, workin' hard, but good da same".

Marcellus' eyes shifted away from Zeb to the cobblestones on the ground. "Yo' money come in real handy, Zeb. I 'preech ate dat so much".

Zeb searched for words to say, to ease Marcellus burden of guilt. He knew how badly his cousin felt. Marcellus, Aunt Virtue, and Uncle Sanders, with his bad back, worked like slaves farming, from sun up to sun down, sometimes fifteen hours a day. And they still needed the extra money that Zeb religiously gave to them. Aunt Virtue and Uncle Sanders were born into slavery. Hard work was all they had ever known. But they both swore on their mama and papa's graves, that the price of freedom under this Reconstruction thing, was just as bad. It was just another name for slavery.

A bell sounded, and someone yelled out: *"The Royal Magnolia is approachin'"! "The ship is comin' in"!*

The tolling of the bell continued as cheers and laughter erupted from the excited crowds, turning the already frenzied atmosphere into an endless spin. Women, weaving sweetgrass baskets nearby, began singing melodic spirituals. Groomed, well-dressed children, played games, while their white-aproned maids stood nearby, awaiting the return of fathers who had been away too long. The Royal Magnolia was a massive steam-powered vessel. Powerful and luxurious, it was in a class by itself. Outbound, from Charleston, The Royal Magnolia, had transported long-staple cotton, indigo, rice, tar, corn, and turpentine to the Caribbean and ports of Europe. It had now departed from the shores of England, bringing with it, exotic perfumes and oils, ornate items, beautiful clothing and fabrics, paintings, furniture, and other manufactured goods. The ship made stops at several Caribbean islands before returning to Charleston. The trip from the Port of Bridgetown in Barbados, to the Port of Charleston, alone, took more than a month.

For most of the black men gathered at the dock this morning, the return of the Royal Magnolia steamer offered decent pay for long, hard, and grueling work. For Charleston's high society, it meant the return of family members, friends, and acquaintances, bringing with them, lots of beautiful garments and precious goods. Local merchants were eager to unload their cargo from England and the West Indies. For Cecile Huntington, who was in a family way, she would be welcoming the return of her husband, Thomas Ashley Huntington. These months of separation came at a time when their marriage was already strained, and her pregnancy, plagued with problems, only made matters worse. She had gotten up early to make certain that Zeb looked presentable, as he always did, and was ready to go to the wharf to wait for the vessel to arrive. Even if it meant Zeb had to wait for hours, then so be it. She did not want her husband waiting around on the crowded dock.

It was a dizzying, chaotic sight to behold. And the sun, rising to its afternoon peak, had no mercy on the masses. Wealthy, first-class passengers were yelling at servants and house-hands, who were frantically trying to claim bags and possessions for their employers. With necks stretched upward and outward, limbs battered by tossed boxes and luggage, it was a sea of madness where everyone lost patience and all semblance of sanity. Mr. Huntington and Zeb, both towering figures, whose heads stood well above the crowds, spotted each other immediately. Thomas waved Zeb over, then pulled a white handkerchief out and mopped sweat that dripped from his tanned forehead.

Thomas Huntington was the splitting image of his father's English bloodline, but his skin took on the olive coloring of his Spanish mother. He had grown a beard, and his skin, tanned from the Caribbean sun, glowed, exuding his inner warmth. He was honest, level-headed, and strikingly handsome, with the perfect balance of formal education and common sense. Like Zeb, he stood out from the crowd.

When Zeb reached Thomas, the two men stood head-to-head facing each other in a manner that was reserved, but quietly polite. As always, much to the disdain of his fellow upper-crust Charlestonians, Thomas Huntington extended his hand to Zeb, who returned a strong shake. The men had always had a sense of deep respect for each other, and neither saw any reason to behave anyway other than that. As a matter-of-fact, it was no secret that Thomas

Huntington often preferred the company of Zeb to some of his well-to-do neighbors, who just didn't understand what one of the country's richest men could possibly have in common with a poor black boy from Edisto. His response to curious inquirers was always the same: "Zeb is a man of good character, great intelligence, and more decency than I've ever seen".

"Welcome home, Mr. Huntington. Glad you return safe". Zeb's voice was calm and measured.

Thomas glanced at the ship looming behind them, his eyes looking in the direction where cargo was being unloaded and black passengers from Barbados were disembarking.

"I'm mighty glad to be back home, as well, Zeb. It sure is good to stand on solid ground again. We ran into a big storm a little over a week ago. Slowed that steamer down quite a bit", he sighed.

Thomas' dark, sea-green eyes widened, as he leaned and stared towards the exiting black passengers.

Zeb's eyes followed his boss'.

"If you give me yo' claim tickets, sir, I'll go grab dem bags".

Thomas handed Zeb an envelope, nonchalantly, his eyes still fixed on the passengers streaming from the ship's lower deck.

"The bags can wait, Zeb. I'm actually looking for *someone*".

"*Someone,* Mr. Huntington? Who"?

Zeb couldn't imagine any of Mr. Huntington's acquaintances from Charleston or relatives from Barbados who would ride down below with the black passengers. Curiosity got the best of him.

They both started walking towards the weary passengers getting off.

Finally, a young girl, got off. She was fanning herself with a big straw hat, and held a bundle under her arm. She was the most exotic-looking creature Zeb had ever seen. Even with the wear and tear of the voyage, under terribly uncomfortable conditions, her beauty came through. Zeb's eyes widened. He was speechless and spellbound.

Seeing how Zeb was taken in by her, Thomas smiled, contentedly.

"And she's quite smart, Zeb. *Gar-de-ni-a* will be the perfect addition to the house staff".

"That's a mighty pretty name", Zeb nodded, his eyes glued on the girl.

Thomas was amused, seeing how Gardenia had, within minutes, tamed the towering, imposing Zeb.

"*And...*I have a strong feeling she'll make a great companion for you".

Zeb never heard a word Thomas said, and he never took his eyes off of Gardenia.

They all laughed when her stomach let out a loud, rebellious, hungry groan.

"Zeb, if you gather my bags, I'll go fetch some food for our starving traveler, and we can be on our way", Thomas directed, as he headed towards an elderly black woman nearby, who sold biscuits and homemade preserves.

The day had gone from dewy to simmering in no time. Above, the rays of the southern sun beamed pitilessly over the hustle and bustle of the seaport. Knowing how eager Mr. Huntington was to get home, Zeb and a few of the dock hands quickly loaded his luggage and goods into Mr. Huntington's personal carriage, filled another cart that had been brought along to accommodate all of his goods. Zeb made a nice comfortable space for Gardenia in the back of the carriage that he drove.

On the ride home, Thomas and Zeb talked mostly about plans for their upcoming trip to the Huntington's Edingsville Beach estate on Edisto—a place both men loved and were eager to get back to. As much as he liked Charleston, what Thomas loved more than anywhere, was his impressive, two-story beach home on Edingsville Beach. During his time in Europe, he had painstakingly searched for, and purchased the most exquisite paintings, silverware, china, and artwork he could find, for his cherished vacation home.

Edingsville was where Thomas had spent every summer of his childhood. They'd be heading there in just a few weeks.

Gardenia took in all of the sights and sounds, quietly marveling at the stately mansions that sat at the back of endless, colorful gardens. The well-dressed ladies, who sat fanning themselves, on wide porches. It was all so breathtakingly beautiful. But she felt so alone. She was a stranger here, in a strange place, with no family, and no friends.

Thomas Huntington had saved her life. He had managed to rescue her from the long work days, and cruel, harsh, treatment by his brother and sister-in-law. While visiting them on their sugar plantation in Barbados, Thomas showered them with beautiful gifts from Europe, and was finally able to persuade them to let him bring Gardenia to Charleston to help with his pregnant wife, Cecile. For that, Gardenia was eternally grateful. She prayed and hoped that she would like this new world.

"This yo' new home", Zeb grinned, nodding his head towards the house.

A loud, joyous scream rang out as Sepia, a brown-skinned woman came running towards the carriage.

"Tanks Gawd you git back safe, Mister Huntington! Tanks Gawd!"

Thomas descended the carriage, and beamed.

"Tell me Sepia, how's it everyone keeps getting older, except you? Now, you haven't gone and given your soul to the devil, have you?", he teased.

Sepia smiled, proudly.

"No suh. Dat debil don' wan' nuttin' a me. I dun cuss him comin' an' goin'. Him skared a me!"

Laughter rang across the yard, as several house hands came out and began unloading the carriage and carts.

Thomas stood in the yard, and took in a long, deep breath. The familiar sound of a window being unlatched echoed from above. His eyes stared up at the second story of the house, where curtains parted, revealing a big bay window. It was shadowy inside, but he knew that Cecile was there. He could feel her presence, and hoped that she would greet him with a smile, and a few warm words. Thomas' smile faded, as the heavy curtains slowly closed, and the shadowy figure disappeared into the room.

It had been months since he'd seen his wife, and Thomas was not about to let her eyes see him unshaven and unkempt. While he shaved and bathed, Sepia and the other housemaids were busy setting the formal dining room table with all of his favorite foods. There was savory she-crab soup, red rice cooked with shrimp, tomatoes, sweet peppers and onions, fried okra and corn, and a saddle of cured venison, with roasted chestnuts and fresh herbs. Her buttery peach cobbler, covered with heavy, rich cream, was Thomas' favorite dessert.

That evening, when Mr. and Mrs. Thomas Huntington came together to dine, for the first time in months, they greeted each other with a cordial kiss on each cheek. Thomas did most of the talking, while Cecile listened, nodded, and smiled, periodically, their eyes, almost always avoiding the other's.

The Huntingtons were very private, reserved people who did not socialize much with Charleston's elite. Few words were ever exchanged between them. Yet, each clearly knew and understood what was expected of the other, and went about doing so, without question. With the exception of Sepia's occasional outcries and exclamations, it was an eerily quiet household, one that felt more like a family of distant relatives, than it did a young couple who was expecting the birth of their child.

Thomas Huntington was a gentleman, a man who could tame and seduce the most difficult of human beings. He could convince savvied businessmen to see his point of view. And now, at the age of twenty-eight, he had mastered the art of his family's gemstone empire, monopolizing the country's gold, diamond, pearl, and precious gemstones industry. It was no secret that he had always been the favorite son and grandson, albeit, the younger. For, within several years, after taking over at the helm, from his ailing father, Thomas had expanded the company across several continents, and had more than tripled the value of his family's business. In fact, he had accomplished more in a few years than his father and grandfather had done since the inception of the business. Still, he remained calm and humble, with a strong, but quite sense of dignity. And yet, with all that he had accomplished, there was one thing that he could not touch, reach, or understand—Cecile.

So cold and distant was she, that Thomas often wondered how they had ever made it to the alter. This tall, Nordic creature, moved ghost-like, throughout their Charleston mansion. Clear, ice-blue eyes lit her face, while a mane of reddish-blonde corn-silk, cascaded down her back. So seldom had her thin lips known the pleasure of a smile. Thomas had reached out to her so many times, and in so many ways. He had tried desperately to touch her, to love her, to make her feel his love. But nothing he did made her happy. After their first child was stillborn, Cecile, herself had crawled into a dark place, not unlike death. In his efforts to make her happy, Thomas showered her with rare jewelry, beautiful, expensive dresses, and exotic gifts. She had an enviable collection of perfumes, body oils and sweet soaps. Yet, Cecile remained unaffected, and seemed to become more and more distant. She was the one thing in his life that was untouchable, and unobtainable.

In the days and weeks following Thomas's return, the entire household was abuzz with the excitement of preparing for the move to Edingsville for the summer. Sepia and the rest of the house servants had welcomed Gardenia with opened arms, and in no time, the exotic girl with the strange way of speaking, had won everyone's heart, especially Zeb's. Being the trained nurse that she was, Gardenia spent most of her days taking care of Cecile's needs, keeping her comfortable, and seeing to it that all of her necessary clothing, accessories, and medicines were close at hand. She was personally responsible for Cecile, gathering, packing, and properly labeling all essential items for the frail, pregnant woman, who spent most of her time in bed.

When she wasn't taking care of Cecile, Gardenia and Zeb often found themselves working closely together, inside and outside of the house. It was Zeb who drove Gardenia to the marketplaces to shop for food and household items. And he took her to the apothecary, to pick up tonics and salves for Cecile. Zeb and Gardenia enjoyed each other's company, and sharing these errands gave them private time together. These were moments that they both always looked forward to. And it gave them time away from the prying eyes of Sepia and the other servants.

The Sunday before they left for Edingsville, Gardenia and Zeb took the long way back to the house, after attending church services. They strolled slowly along the Battery near the Charleston harbor, lit beautifully by the sun. Zeb told her stories about Aunt Virtue, Uncle Sanders, and his cousin Marcellus. And talked about growing up on Edisto. Gardenia shared stories about her childhood days in the village of St. James Town, in Barbados. They talked and laughed, and were thrilled each time they stumbled upon another similarity between the people of Edisto and the people of Barbados. The two islands were more than three thousand miles apart, and yet, like Gardenia and Zeb, they were so much alike, and, alike in all of the right ways.

The day came when the Huntingtons left Charleston and were bound for Edingsville. Sepia and several servants had gone ahead several days earlier, to clean and prepare the elegant beach home. They boarded the *Planter Steamboat* from Charleston Harbor, and landed at Edingsville just as the sun was setting. Edingsville was an exclusive summer resort for wealthy plantation owners, and Charleston's and Savannah's aristocracy. During hot weather, the rich left their estates behind, and, remained until the start of winter. Edingsville gave them an escape from malarial mosquitoes, and other heat borne diseases. Whites were susceptible to a dangerous form of malaria that many blacks were immuned to. Thomas understood well, that his wife, who would soon give birth to their child, already had one foot in the grave. Edingsville was a refuge from the heat and humidity. The cool, ocean breeze would comfort her. And he hoped the 'salt and pines' would make her feel better.

The beach was long, with pretty white sand. A wide, dirt road lead to the Huntington's magnificent front row estate. A two-story abode, with a chimney, and a spacious wrap-around veranda, the house was situated facing the endless Atlantic Ocean. It was an impressive community for the elite and well-heeled. Thomas and Cecile would attend the Presbyterian church on the strand. There were boathouses, a billiard saloon, and fresh water cisterns. Thomas marveled at the beauty and serenity of Edingsville. It was where he had spent all of his childhood summers. This was where his heart was. And he was happy to be back.

Gardenia felt at home, the moment she stepped foot onto Edisto. It was all and more than Zeb said it would be. When she met Aunt Virtue, Uncle Sanders, and Marcellus, it felt as if she'd known them forever. There was a sense of familiarity that made her feel comfortable with them. She and Aunt Virtue became best friends within moments of meeting each other. The trees, flowers, birds, and smells of Edisto, all reminded her of home. Even Uncle Sanders' stories and tales had a familiar ring to them. The way Aunt Virtue collected and dried her spices, teas, herbs, and medicinal roots—done exactly the way they were done in Barbados. In her heart, Gardenia knew that Edisto was where she belonged. She had been brought across wide waters for a reason.

Two weeks after arriving on Edisto, Gardenia, Aunt Virtue, and Sepia *"ketch'd"* a healthy baby boy, as he tumbled out from Cecile's womb. As the proud father held his son, for the first time in a long while, Thomas Huntington saw and felt the warmth of his wife's smile.

A month later, Zeb and Gardenia were united in holy matrimony. They made their home on Edisto Island.

Samson an' Gallileah

Now, de ol' folks say dem two bin cuss from de staa't. Yes-suh!

Samson Green was born to break hearts. And that he did. He was one of the tallest men on Edisto, and by far, the best looking man anyone had ever laid eyes on this side of Charleston. He was what folks called a 'brass ankle", meaning he had the mixed bloods of Black, White and Indian surging all through those veins of his. Square-jawed with a mouthful of pearly white teeth, he had a smile that could, and did melt many hearts.

They say the way he ended up with the name Samson, was because, well, he was the *son* of Perlina and Big Sam. In fact, he was their *only son* and *only child.* Now, aiming to honor three generations of men in his family, Big Sam took all of those given-names, rolled them together into one long name, and cursed his son with a name so long, no one could ever get through it in one breath. Not even Big Sam. *Yes-suh!* Samson was a name that boy took to *"jes'like w'ite on rice"*. You see, even as a young boy, he was already full of himself, and had figured out early on that he was going to do his best to live up to such a strong and virile name.

With all of his God-given gifts, Samson was, no doubt, a ladies' man—the kind most men envied. He had a smooth way with words, and an even smoother way with the ladies. And as for those smoldering brown bedroom eyes, well, they did far more than their share of wandering.

Now, Samson's wandering eyes might not have been a problem had it not been for the fact that he was...well...a married man. He was indeed, united in holy matrimony and wed-lock, and had *"done jump dat brum"* with a sweet and gentle woman named Gallileah. Everyone on Edisto just called her *Gallie*. Ol' folks remember how pretty Gallie was when Samson first *"bin keepin' comp'ny"* with her. She was tall and lean. Most of the older women said she was too thin, but they figured she would *"plumpin' up afta' birthin' some chillun"*.

Gallie had beautiful cinnamon brown skin, and a full head of heavy black hair that framed her gloriously high cheekbones. She had lips that curled when she smiled, and a set of even, white teeth. Her eyes, which slanted upwards at the corners, were catlike and mesmerizing. She was warm and soft-spoken, with that rapid sing-song lilt to her speech that was common with Geechee folk from St. Helena Island and Beaufort. Everyone liked her. Back then, Samson never let the poor girl out of his sight or arms. Nearly stifled her. But to the curious folks on Edisto, Gallie was a bit of a mystery. Seems the only thing they knew about her for sure, was that she was from St. Helena Island, where she still had close relations and family ties. Ever since her mama, papa, and sister drowned in the big hurricane of 1893, her maternal grand mother, Mama Ola had raised her.

Samson and Gallie met in nineteen aught seven at Accommodation Wharf in the busy seaport of Charleston. They were both waiting to board the Merchant Steamboat, a sailing vessel that carried passengers and cargo between Charleston and the sea islands. Samson was returning to Edisto after having worked for several days as an extra hand loading and unloading cargo on the docks. Gallie, having taken care of some important matters in Charleston for her Mama Ola, was returning to St. Helena Island. Amidst all the noise, confusion, and the bustle, Gallie stood out from the crowd. She was breathtakingly beautiful, and she took Samson's breath away from him the moment he laid his eagle eyes on her. He had to have her. He was twenty-two years old, and she, barely seventeen.

Freight and cargo were loaded onto the steamboat first. This was followed by well-dressed white people who cheerfully made their way onto the first deck. Finally, Black passengers, packed tightly, who had waited patiently, were ordered to board the vessel. Eager to get to the girl before someone else did, Samson pushed through the crowds, and quickly grabbed her two large burlap bags, just as she was reaching for them.

"You's too purdee an' slight to be liffin' deese yah hebby bags." He grinned, and picked up both bags.

"Samson my name."

She smiled. "Gal-li-le-ah my name. Jes' call me Gallie, fo' short."

Samson was completely smitten by the enchanting girl, whose hypnotic eyes lit up like stars on a dark night. Her rich, rapid, sing-song voice, told him she was either from St. Helena Island or Beaufort. They both spoke Gullah, but folks on Edisto spoke Gullah at a much slower pace than folks from the Beaufort area. The untrained ears of strangers would never have noticed the difference. Samson and Gallie talked and laughed, and made plans to meet the following week. When the Merchant Steamer docked at Steamboat Landing Wharf on Edisto, Samson hung around as long as possible, talking to Gallie before being ordered by a crewman to leave the vessel. Gallie could feel her heart beating against her chest. She was smitten by the tall, handsome man. As the steamboat hummed towards St. Helena Island, the only thing Gallie thought of was Samson Green.

What Samson learned about Gallie was that her mama, papa, and a sister were all killed in the storm, that dreadful night, the 27th of August, in 1893. Old folks say hundreds of poor Black people living in tenant houses and shanties on the sea islands of Georgia and South Carolina, were awaken by a surging wall of water in the middle of the night—their lives, families, and homes, all washed to sea in watery graves. Gallie, a child of three at the time, and her grandmother, Mama Ola, had managed to survive the devastating tidal surge by climbing way up into a tall, live oak tree, where Mama Ola held on to her precious grandchild for hours, as the evil winds and rain tortured them unmercifully. Throughout that hellish night, they had both refused to give in to the raging storm. There were times when Mama Ola felt as if the child was, in some way or another, protecting them both from a horrible and certain death. When it was all over, and the thirty-foot tidal surge had gone back to sea, there were bodies strewn all around them. Her mama and papa's bodies were found tangled among some branches and seaweeds. Sadly, her sister, a year older than Gallie, was never found. She was believed to have been washed away to sea, but Gallie felt that her sister would one day return.

The day Samson and Gallie were married, and jumped over that sweetgrass broom at Olde Baptist Church, folks say *"ol' man devil"* must have been beating his wife some bad. They say just as the wedding got underway, *"nuttin' but de rain come pourin' down. An' all along, dat sun jes' keep on a-shinnin'."* Ol' folks say that devil beating his wife was one sign that was clear as day.

Now, Samson was the only child that Perlina and Big Sam were blessed with. His mama, Perlina, spoilt him rotten, and his papa, Big Sam, ruined the boy, and probably cursed him with that long name he gave him. But folks believed that Samson was plain lonely growing up all by himself, and maybe that was why he always said that when he grew up and got married, he wanted to have *"a house full a boy chillun, 'cos* dem *gal chillun was trouble."* Samson wanted to waste no time going about making his sons, and Gallie, loving Samson as much as she did, wanted nothing more than to please him.

One day while Gallie was in the backyard pumping water, her hands slipped, and the long handle of the pump struck her belly with so much force that it nearly knocked her off of her feet. There was an awful pain, then an aura, as streams of hot, red blood rushed down her legs, her long skirt stained soaked. She let out an earth shattering scream. Their dog Swee' Tater, started barking and ran to find Samson. Samson ran to Gallie, lifted her into his arms and yelled for help.

"Please! Somebody! Come help me yah! Gallie da bleedin' my boy chile rite from she belly!"

In no time, neighbors were coming to help. But by the time, Mis' Maybelle arrived, Samson and the neighbors knew it was too late to save his unborn child. Mis' Maybelle was one of the oldest and most experienced grannies on Edisto. Aside from being a granny midwife, she was revered and well-respected as a "wise woman" throughout the sea islands. Her grandson had barely parked the mule and wagon, when Mis' Maybelle, her big, leather tote bag held firmly in her hand, descended from the wagon and ran into Gallie's bedroom. Gallie's little cabin was clean and orderly, so the granny midwife went to doing what she needed to do right away. She used a preparation of curing sweetgrass and herbs she'd brought with her to stop Gallie's bleeding, and to cleanse her. One of the neighboring women who usually helped out grannies, knew what to do, and had already placed a big pot of water on the stove to be heated. Boiling hot water in a kettle would be poured over special roots and leaves that Mis' Maybelle had brought along. The women then forced the grief-stricken Gallie to drink the bitter tea. As she was accustomed to doing with new mothers, or with women who had had the misfortune of losing their unborn babies, Mis' Maybelle came prepared to spend the next week or so, right there, nursing Gallie, taking care that she was out of the woods and well on her way to healing.

The day before she left their home, Mis' Maybelle brought Samson to Gallie's bedside. She gently placed Gallie's hand into Samson's, and spoke to them in a soft, motherly way.

"Wid time, Gallie gon' git betta. She gon' heal. But I don' tink she gon' eva be strong 'nuf to mak' mo' chillun."

Samson's knees buckled and his head dropped.

Gallie shook her head in disbelief, as tears welled in her sad eyes.

Mis' Maybelle gave Samson a long, stern glance and waited for him to look at her before she continued.

"Dis chile gon' need you to be dare fo' her now mo' dan eva ba fo'. Now 'memba', y'all done jump dat brum togetta in chu'ch an' dat means you is one now. Be good to each otter an' tak care each otter."

With those parting words, the midwife felt Gallie's forehead to make sure there was no fever, then patted her gently on the head. As payment for her services, Samson handed the granny midwife fabric, fresh string beans, sweet potatoes, and a small basket of fresh eggs he'd collected from the chicken coop out back. As he handed her the bundle of goods, their eyes locked momentarily. The old woman spoke not another word, for her eyes said it all. She simply nodded and left.

In the weeks that followed, neighborhood women took turns visiting and checking in on Gallie. Gradually, her strength returned and she was up and about again. Gallie knew that Mis' Maybelle was one of those gifted women who had been *"called upon"* to heal others. She trusted and respected her. But deep down inside, she wanted the wise woman to be wrong, just this once. She had hoped and prayed that she would still be able to give Samson the children he wanted.

Gallie went to every healer and midwife on Edisto, but no one could *"fix"* her. She had even thought about going to Beaufort for fertility help, but she was afraid that word of it would get back to Mama Ola. That was the last thing she wanted or needed. The old woman did not take well to Samson, and likewise, he had no affection for her. There was something about Samson that rubbed her the wrong way. It was a shame that although Gallie had begged Samson to let her elderly and frail gran'mama come live with them on Edisto, he had stubbornly refused, and Gallie was caught in the middle, between them. From time-to-time, she would walk the half-mile to Steamboat Landing Wharf, and take the steamboat to St. Helena to visit Mama Ola. It had be awhile since she'd seen her, and Gallie knew how clever her gran'mama was. She knew that one long look at her, would be all the old woman needed to do, and she would know exactly what had happened. Even worse,

Gallie was beginning to feel that Samson was drifting away from her and their home. It crossed her mind several times that there were "things" she could do, but she was afraid that it might frighten Samson and chase him away completely. She was still too afraid, unwilling, and not ready to use what Mama Ola called *"dat speshil t'ing"*.

One day, Gallie got a visit from a young lady named Lavinia Luvell. Lavinia was born in Barbados, but had come to Edisto as a little girl with her mother, Flora. Flora had worked as a live-in nurse and healer in the big house on a sugarcane plantation in Barbados. Educated and trained as a nurse in Europe, Flora was from a long line of healers and baby "ketchers". While on a business trip in Barbados, a wealthy Edisto landowner was so impressed by Flora's knowledge, mannerisms, and expertise, that plans were immediately made to have her and her 4-year-old daughter Lavinia, return with him to Edisto, where, as a *"Swonga"*, she would work and live in the big house as a trained nurse. Flora was just what he needed to take care of his workers.

Lavinia had learned everything she knew about *"ketchin' babies"* and healing from her mother and grandmother. Moreover, Lavinia was said to have been born with a *veil* on her face, and was, by all accounts, a very special healer. Lavinia was much younger than the other grannies and midwives on the island, and well-educated. She could read and write—skills that had been deemed illegal and denied to the older grannies. Lavinia was lean, with keen features. She had a long neck that sat gracefully on her sculptured shoulders. Long arms, slender hands, and piercing eyes that seemed to look deep inside

Gallie's soul. There was a calming aura about her that made Gallie feel safe and comfortable, as if they'd known each other forever, although they'd only seen each other occasionally at church. Interestingly, it was Mis' Maybelle who had urged Gallie to meet with Lavinia. Gallie hoped that Lavinia would be able to *fix* her infertility.

Lavinia smiled slightly and kept her eyes firmly on Gallie as she gently slid into a wooden chair at the small table.

"May I have a glass of water...from the pump, please? I'll need to see things as clearly as possible."

"Course." Gallie took a glass jar from the top shelf of the cupboard and quickly ran outside to the pump. She returned and wiped the glass of cold water with her apron before handing it to Lavinia.

Lavinia placed the glass of water half-way between them on the table.

"Please stand, and place the palms of your opened hands over the water."

Gallie was nervous, and her hands trembled as she raised them above the glass of water.

Lavinia took Gallie's hands and slowly lowered them towards the water. Just as Gallie's hands were about the touch the rim of the glass, she screamed and jerked away from Lavinia's grasp.

"It hotta' dan fire! Dat burn my han' mo dan fire!" Gallie's eyes widened as she rubbed her hands together and blew into them to cool the burning.

Lavinia realized that her hands were also burning, and stared curiously at Gallie for awhile. When she spoke her words were as clear and cool as the glass of water.

"Because there is fire. You're sleeping in a burning bed." Lavinia cleared her throat and leaned back into the chair.

Lavinia was her last hope, and Gallie knew that she was about to hear something she had hoped not to hear. Deep down inside, she knew that she would never be able to give Samson the children he wanted. It was something she'd sensed for awhile. Somehow, when Lavinia spoke to her, it all seemed okay. As a matter-of-fact, it felt right.

Lavinia rose from the chair as gracefully as she had slid into it. She paused and took a deep breath.

"He will father children, but you will never be able to give him children," she sighed.

"Be sure to throw the water out before your husband returns home tonight. And please, go spend sometime with your gran'mama."

Gallie shook her head, but thought it was strange since she hadn't mentioned Mama Ola at all to Lavinia.

Lavinia put her arms around Gallie and patted her reassuringly on the back, before turning to leave.

"Remember, everything happens for a reason. In life, our paths are made even before we're born."

Standing in the doorway, Gallie watched as Lavinia made her way over to the sprawling Angel Oak tree where she had left her mule and wagon. She'd never seen any woman walk as elegantly as Lavinia did, Gallie thought. It was as if she floated on air, with her feet barely touching the ground. Her eyes followed Lavinia's hands as she carefully unwrapped the reins that had been loosely draped around the post. Samson had built the pine post long enough to accommodate several mules and carts. Without the slightest effort, Lavinia mounted the small wagon, then turned and waved goodbye. Gallie waited in the doorway until she could no longer see any sign of Lavinia. She took a long, deep breath, then slowly exhaled.

In the months and years that followed, Gallie busied herself with cooking, sewing, gardening, canning, quilting, and whatever she could do to make their home a pleasant and beautiful place to live. She made the most handsome suits, shirts, and ties for Samson. Tried, as she did, it seemed there was nothing she could do to make Samson happy. The more she tried to please him, the more distant he became. Gallie soon learned how cold and mean he could be. Gallie loved Samson completely, and it destroyed her that, not only did he reject her delicate, amorous advances, but there were times when he looked at her with hate in his eyes. She would soon learn just how cold and mean her husband had become.

They hadn't talked about it, but in her gut, Gallie knew that her husband was seeing other women. There were so many nights when he returned home long after she had retired to bed. Other times, he made it back home barely before day clean, just in time for one of her tasty breakfasts. Stories about Samson's infidelities and dalliances were rampant. There were times when, he even flirted with women in Gallie's presence, after Sunday service, in the churchyard. Even worse, folks on Edisto Island were beginning to whisper and talk about how Samson had been sowing his wild oats all over the land.

Gallie was heartbroken, but she still loved Samson and wanted desperately to save their marriage. She got up early one day while Samson was still asleep. She primped her hair into a pretty style, and got dressed in her best Sunday-go-to-meeting dress. It was a pretty lilac pink, trimmed in fancy, flowing ribbons—the same color she wore on the day she and Samson had first met—ten years ago! How fast the years had gone by. She had just turned twenty-seven years old, but so many long, lonely nights of crying, hurting, and suffering in silence made her feel so much older. Over the years, the rumors, gossip and Samson's torturous silence towards her, had all wreaked havoc on her spirit, and had taken a toll on her looks. She inspected her image in the mirror then went to make breakfast for her husband.

Samson woke to the smell of hot clabber biscuits, thick, buttery grits, smoked bacon ham, and fried eggs. He was bathed and dressed when he came out of the bedroom and over to the kitchen area of their cabin. Gallie had set the table with china they'd gotten as a wedding gift. She hoped it meant something to Samson.

She smiled and gently placed her hand on his shoulder.

"Goodmornin' Samson", she said in her sweetest voice.

"Mornin'" he grumbled without even looking at her. Gallie's heart fell, but as Samson reached for the grits, she got up to help him. At that moment, Samson knocked her hand away, pushed himself away from the table and stood up over her. His enraged body shook uncontrollably, his eyes, glaring, filled with hate and anger. She was afraid of him, of what he might do to her. The red, hot anger that came from him. She braced herself, fearing he would hit her, beat her to death.

"Dat boy o'mine woulda bin nary ten yays ol' by now Gallie! But no! Yo' head bin haad! Yo' jes' had ta go an' pump dat bucket o' wadda. Dat pump kick yo' belly an' kill my boy chile jes' like so!"

Gallie fell into the chair, shocked and speechless. Her body and mind went numb as she tried to grasp how, after all of these years, Samson still blamed her for losing their unborn child. Didn't he know how guilty she felt? How much she hated herself for what had happened? It was a terrible accident that day, and losing their baby had been the most painful thing she'd ever experienced. Tears flooded her face, but somehow she found the strength to get up, and went over to try to console her grieving husband. As she went to embrace him, Samson's hand suddenly went up and came down on her with so much force and fury that it knocked her to the floor, several feet away. Her head was pounding, and the room spun around her. In total disbelief, she crept towards the table, grabbed onto it, then pulled herself up. Just as she stood up, Samson leapt across the room. Towering like a giant shadow over her, he struck her over, and over again! Gallie fell to the floor, puking, and bleeding, her body writhing in unbelievable pain. Her dizzy mind, unable to make sense of what had happened. Her heart was still beating, but it was shattered, destroyed, and broken into a million pieces. She felt her body and mind falling, plunging deeper into darkness. At first, she struggled to stay awake. She wanted to get up. Tried to get up. But could not move. Finally, she gave in and closed her eyes.

Day had grown into dusk when Gallie finally came to. Samson was no way in sight. Not only had he beaten her to a pulp and left her lying bruised and bloodied on a rough, splintered floor, but he had left the house, not knowing if she was dead or alive. Gallie's entire body ached as she limped towards the bedroom. A glimpse of her bruised, swollen face in the mirror frightened her so much that she screamed out loud, the pain and hurt echoing throughout the cabin.

It had been a long time since she'd visited her gran'mama Ola, and Gallie needed to get away from Samson. She could no longer bear to look at him. A few weeks before Easter Sunday, Gallie got up early and packed some clothes in her burlap travel bag. She told Samson she had decided to spend some time with her ill gran'mama, but that she'd be back on Edisto to attend Easter Sunrise Service at Olde Baptist Church. It didn't seem to bother Samson that his wife would be gone for such a long time. He never even said good-bye, as she picked up her burlap bag and flung it over her shoulder. Gallie left the house then walked half a mile to Steamboat Landing, where she waited among the growing crowd to board the Merchant Steamboat.

On the ride down to St. Helena, Gallie thought about how wrong things had gone in her marriage. How could so much ruin have come to their lives together? Why did Samson blame her for the loss of their unborn baby? How could he hate her the way he did, when she loved him more than life itself? How could he beat and hit her, and act as if it hadn't happened? She had given all of herself, years of love and time to a man who didn't care enough about her to even say 'good-bye', knowing she'd be gone for weeks. The pain was more than she could bear. But there was something else bothering her. Something that was keeping her awake at night, and eating away at her. It was that little "all knowing voice" deep down inside of her, telling her something she needed to hear.

Over the years, she'd gotten used to the sympathetic glances from other women, the pitying pat on her back, and the whispers and hushed voices of people in church. But it was the rumor about a woman Samson had been involved with, who, upon learning that she was carrying his child, told him about it. Little did the woman know that Samson had already moved on to someone new. When Samson rejected her, and her condition, the poor woman became so distraught that she left home one day without telling anyone where she was going or when she would return. A couple of days later, fishermen found her bloody, beaten body in a floating in the dark, green, murky waters of a creek. Gallie shuddered, and her body went cold when she remembered how Samson had beaten her, and left her bleeding and lying on a rough wooden floor. She shook her head, not wanting to hear what the voice inside was shouting at her. As they neared the dock, the loud humming of the steamboat seemed to drown some of her thoughts. But not her fears. And what Gallie feared most, was that she was living with a stranger. For more than ten years, she had been married to a man she did not know.

Luckily, Mama Ola's house was just a stone's throw away from the dock on St. Helena Island. Gallie crossed Main Road and took one of the narrow, winding paths. It was a short-cut to the house, a small, neat cabin, with a little stoop. The door frame, steps, and wooden window shutters were painted "taint blue", to keep evil spirits at bay. As she came closer to the big yard, Gallie heard Mama Ola singing what sounded more like a chant than a hymn. It was an old chant she hadn't heard in years, but the words came flowing back to her, and she chanted along. Shaded by a cavern of ancient trees, Mama Ola sat calmly in her rocking chair, puffing on a cornstalk tobacco pipe. Above her, silvery gray Spanish moss, the same color of the old woman's thick braids, hung lazily over long, oak tree limbs. Her companion, a keen-eyed black cat, with its hunched back, hovered nearby. Gallie hugged and held her gran'mama, then knelt down on the grass beside her. She was thin and frail, but at the sight of her beloved granddaughter, Viola Aprile Peoples' old eyes lit up like fire. They hugged and held each other tightly. Mama Ola took Gallie's hands and placed two small pouches inside. Gallie knew exactly what they were. More importantly, she knew what they represented, and how powerful they could be, when they were in the hands of the right person, and used for the right reasons. Gallie stood up, then helped the old woman out of her rocking chair. She looked into her gran'mama's tired, but wise eyes, and together, they spoke these words:

"One good, one evil, between them we stand".

With that, Gallie knew that her time and calling had come. In the days and nights that followed, Gallie and her gran'mama made the most of their time together, side-by-side, one the wise teacher, the other, the eager student, as age-old wisdom, practices, knowledge, and ancient wit from the Motherland, was once again passed from one generation to the next.

From the moment Mama Ola first ketch Gallie from her daughter on that cold January night, she knew right there and then that there was something special about her. She was born with eyes wide open and a cry that was so strong nearly everyone on St. Helena Island could hear her! Ever since she was knee-high to a grasshopper, she was always right there next to Mama Ola, watching her, studying her craft, taking in everything she saw, her young mind filled with information that was older than time itself. As a child, Mama Ola had taken her into the swamps and savannas of Beaufort and St. Helena Island, and shown her where and how to find certain healing roots, herbs, and leaves. She learned what times of the year to gather and dry roots, leaves, and berries, and how to prepare and use them. She went along when Mama Ola made house calls to the sick, and helped her when it was time to ketch babies. She was only nine years old when Mama Ola trusted her enough to let her ketch her first baby!

There were so many wonderful things that her gran'mama had taught her. She was proud to be Viola Aprile Peoples' granddaughter, and wanted desperately to live up to the old woman's expectations. Her gran'mama had a reputation as a well-loved and trusted healer and spiritual reader. She was a root woman who had always used her knowledge for good. Gallie couldn't think of a time when her gran'mama had ever done anything mean or evil to anyone. And whenever folks came to her with wicked intents, Mama Ola would send them on their way with a solid prayer and a chant.

But there was a secret that her gran'mama kept from everyone, a secret that only she and Gallie knew about. It was something that had frightened her so much as a child, that she had blocked it out of her young mind, and buried it deep down inside. It was what Mama Ola called *"dat speshil t'ing"*. Mama Ola told her it was nothing to be ashamed of, and that she could never completely run away from it *"cause dat bin Gawd-gibben"*. It was something she was born with, and was as much a part of who she was as the blood that flowed through her veins. Gallie knew that her gran'mama was right. She also knew that, when the time was right, she would come to terms with it, and one day, again, use that special power. Mama Ola always knew that, even as a baby, Gallie did certain things that were unusual and unnatural. Gallie was barely four years old when her gran'mama saw what Gallie could do when her cat eyes *latch* on to you.

Early one morning, after they had eaten a hearty breakfast, Mama Ola stepped outside and took several deep breaths. The rank smell of the salt marsh told her the tide was low, and that the creeks were brimming with fat oysters, crab and shrimp. She frowned at the thought of digging into the stink, slimy mud, but she and Gallie both loved steamed crab and shrimp. The murky, pluff mud would be at least ankle deep. They donned their fishermen boots, gathered a cast net and bucket, and journeyed to the creek behind the house. When they returned home, they were greeted by a large diamondback rattlesnake curled in the front yard near the steps. It was busy shedding skin it had outgrown. Startled by them, the snake raised its angry head and was about to strike, when its vicious eyes locked with Gallie's eyes. Charmed, the serpent became motionless, and slowly began recoiling, and continued until it had wrapped itself into a little, furry, black ball. Mama Ola could not believe what she was seeing with her own two eyes! She had only heard stories about certain people who had the power to charm and change things with their minds and eyes. But she had never actually witnessed it. When the rattlesnake uncoiled, it was no longer a snake, but instead, a little black kitten! The poisonous snake had disappeared, and in its place, a frightened kitten sprung up. Mama Ola watched as Gallie patted the kitten playfully on its head, before it scampered off. Realizing what had happened, Gallie turned to Mama Ola, her tear-filled eyes flooded with the look of shock and shame. She ran crying into the house. Whenever Mama Ola tried to talk to her about what had happened, Gallie would withdraw for days, sobbing hysterically, not eating and not talking. Finally, Mama Ola had decided to leave it alone.

    The weeks she'd spent with her gran'mama were filled with excitement, memories, tears, and laughter. The time had gone by quickly, and Gallie was happy to see how spending time with Mama Ola had lifted her spirits and the way she looked. It was as if her gran'mama had been given a new lease on life. As for Gallie, her spirit had been renewed, and in many ways, she had been reborn. She was ready to return to Edisto and to Samson.

It was late Saturday evening when Gallie returned to Edisto. As she had expected, Samson was not at home. She unpacked and tidied the cabin. She prepared a wonderful supper of sweet potatoes, fried pork, rice, and gravy for her husband. She bathed, and went to bed. She was in such a deep sleep that she didn't hear Samson when he came in, drunk, and devoured his supper.

It was dark when the couple arose well before sun-up on Easter Sunday morning. They ate breakfast, then got ready for the early morning service. Samson got dressed in his best Sunday-go-to-meeting suit, a white shirt with a high collar, and a handsome necktie. They were all gifts his wife had lovingly made for him. Gallie hummed softly as she stepped into a pretty pink, dress. She pulled her hair back into an elegant bun, and carefully placed a lacy hat on her head. Finally, she slid her hands into a pair of gloves that matched her hat. The hat and gloves were gifts from Mama Ola. From the corner of her eyes, Gallie got a glimpse of Samson, as he stood admiring her. She turned and smiled affectionately at her wayward husband. Samson's eyes seemed to soften as he led the way out of the house. They climbed into the mule-drawn wagon and headed to Olde Baptist Church. Little did Samson know, that on this day, his life would be changed forever.

It was Easter Sunday, 1918, and Olde Baptist Church was packed to the rafters—filled with faithful, God-fearing congregants dressed in their very best. They had all come to worship in fellowship, and to witness the first rays before sunrise. On this early Easter morn, a special visiting minister had been invited to deliver the sunrise sermon. His name was The Right Reverend Wright. Now, folks on Edisto didn't know much about The Right Reverend Wright, except that he had traveled far and wide, and it was guaranteed that he would bring the mighty to their knees! Ol' folks say he delivered one thunderous, soul-shaking sermon that had church folk shouting and rolling down the aisles. He based his stirring sermon on the 6th and 7th Commandments: *"Thou Shalt Not Kill"* and *"Thou Shalt Not Commit Adultery"*. Elders said that his powerful homily had the good church folk shouting and jumping for glory. And before he was done, he asked the congregants to fall down on their knees in prayer. When the praying was done, the believers rose to shake hands with their neighbors. Gallie spoke briefly with some of the women, hugging and embracing them. Then she hurried out of the church. Samson watched, as his wife, half-way through the old cemetery, turned and smiled seductively at him. He ran down the steps of the church, and followed her, through the shaded cemetery, filled with towering, tombstones, ancient marble crosses, and tilted tabby headstones. Intoxicated by the sweet smell of magnolia, that seemed to come from everywhere, Samson hurried, so not to lose sight of Gallie's pretty pink dress, that danced about her like wings that were caught in a storm. Why did this all seem so scary, yet familiar to Samson? All of it felt like a wild and strange dream to him. Before he knew it, he was running through the densely wooded thicket, and boggy swamps. He stopped in his tracks when he saw Gallie standing near the bank of a creek. Her back was turned, and she had stopped running. Everything was still and calm, except her dress, which danced wildly about her, in every direction. Samson could not make any sense out of what was happening. Why was her dress whipping to and fro' when there wasn't the slightest breeze in the air? There were no leaves rustling, no moss swaying from tree limbs, and no ripples in the creek. When he called out to Gallie, he could not believe the gibberish that came from his mouth. He was confused and delirious. As he walked towards Gallie, he felt himself falling closer and closer towards the ground. By the time he reached Gallie's side, he was crawling on his hands and knees, more like an animal than a human. At that very moment, Gallie turned to face Samson. Looking down at him, he realized that it was no longer Gallie's face, but the face of his dead lover, the woman whom he had beaten, then drowned after she had told him about her pregnancy. Samson became more and more confused and frightened. He tried to stand, but could not. When he tried to speak the thoughts that were inside his head, he discovered that he could only bark and woof.

Samson shook his head. This was a bad dream, one that he wanted to end. He looked up at the woman standing over him, tears streaming down his face. He tried hard to say he was sorry, and begged her for forgiveness. But again, there was only the sound of a bark that came out of his mouth.

When Gallie's face reappeared, she spoke in her sweetest voice:

"My sister's body was never found after the storm because she survived. By the time she was rescued that night, her mind and body were so beaten and addled, she had no recollection of who she was. She was taken in by a family who moved back to Boston. It took her years to put the pieces together. She came back south to find her family. Instead, she ran into you. The day the fishermen pulled her bruised body from the creek, Mama Ola was called on to see if she could identify the poor soul. She nearly fainted when she saw the star-shaped birthmark near the woman's elbow. Mama Ola knew it was her grand-daughter, my sister.

Gallie stared down at Samson and smiled sweetly. She turned, and began humming as she headed back towards the church. Samson groaned, and scratched, and woofed and barked. As they came through the cemetery, folks in the churchyard turned and watched silently as Gallie approached, with Samson, following behind, on all fours. No one could believe what they were seeing, yet, no one uttered a word. The Right Reverend Wright helped Gallie as she mounted her wagon. He spoke not a word. Simply lifted his hat to her and nodded. As he climbed into his own buggy, and readied to leave, he smiled broadly at the good church folks standing in the yard.

"Well, looks to me like the Lord's will has been done. I'se got one mo' stop to mak' down in Daufauskie. You folks on Edisto be good to one anodder." And with those parting words, The Right Reverend Wright left Edisto.

Gallie was prim and proper as she sat in the wagon. Samson barked. By now, all of his human features had changed so much that he resembled a fox hunter. A gasp came from the congregants as the obedient dog leapt into the wagon, and Gallie patted him gently on his head. Gallie waved, smiled sweetly, and left.

Now, the people of Edisto knowing and understanding such things, never once bothered Gallie to explain what had befallen upon Samson. They figured Gallie knew exactly what she was doing. And as for Samson Green? Dem ol' folks say:

"Him git wah him had comin' to him".

Dat Cryin' Chile

For two nights now, the residents of Ravenswood had been awakened by the agonizing cries that were surely coming from a child. Concerned that the infant might be lost and wandering helplessly in the swamps, several young neighborhood men decided to search the wooded areas. The jungle-like forest was filled with over-sized bobcats and other wild-life, some of them believed to be rabic. Under the canopy of a dark, ominous sky, armed and dressed in hunter's clothing, the determined young men ventured deep into the thickets. The night air crackled with the sound of their heavy boots hitting against dried leaves and twigs that carpeted the ground. As they strode further into the quagmire, again they heard the sound of a child, crying, pleading desperately to be found. The young men in the search party were convinced that someone's baby had surely escaped the safety of its home, while his parents slept, unwittingly. The crying got louder and louder. It came to a pitch, and then, suddenly stopped. Beyond them, just in view, stood two shadowy figures—Primus and Cuffy Smalls—two of the oldest living men on the island. As they lifted their lanterns to light the night, the youngsters immediately recognized the elders and greeted them.

"Good ev'nin' Mister Primus, Mister Cuffy", said one.

"Guess yall's saachin' fo' dat cryin' chile same like we", another added.

Primus and Cuffy raised their lanterns to get a better look at the faces in the group. After surveying the young men, Primus and Cuffy exchanged glances. Primus shifted his lantern, and slowly removed the corn cob tobacco pipe from his mouth. He spoke in a heavy, raspy voice, laden with years.

"When word reach me an' Cuffy dat hunnah bin saachin' fo' dat cryin' chile, we figa' bes' come an' stop hunnah rite in yo' trac".

Confused and waiting for an explanation, the men shifted, then looked curiously at Primus and Cuffy.

'Mister Primus, we's fixin' ta fin' dat baby t'nite".

At that moment, a cold wind suddenly blew through the trees, rustling leaves and branches. Then it happened again. At first it was distant, but then the crying got closer and closer, louder and louder, echoing throughout the forest. The men all lifted their lanterns, one higher than the other, their heads turning every which way, eyes, wide open, looking, and searching, hoping to discover the small, tear-drenched face of a child nearby. The crying was so intense and deafening, the men had to cover their ears. The crying stopped as suddenly as it had started. The cold wind ceased, and the forest went silent. For awhile, no one moved or spoke a word. Cuffy, shaken and nervous, stared at Primus.

"Well, go on, Primus. Tellum! Tellum eb'ry t'ing. Dem boys ought to know jes' wha' happen"!

"Wha' ya mean by eb'ry t'ing wha' happen?", one of the men asked, his eyes shifting wildly from Cuffy to Primus.

Primus placed his lantern on the ground, uneasily, then patted his pockets in search of matches. His bent, tobacco-stained fingers fumbled, as he carefully packed and lit his pipe. He needed time to collect his thoughts and get his words together. Primus drew gently on his pipe, taking short puffs, then blowing back through the corn cob. His old eyes gleamed and narrowed to slits. As little clouds of smoke drifted away from his pipe, so did Primus' memory-- back to that unforgettable night, long, long ago.

It happened upon a dark and chilly Christmas Eve, in nineteen aught two. Maribelle and Seymour Brewster, a young couple, having left the hustle and bustle of big city life behind them, had recently moved into their modest cabin in the quiet Ravenswood hamlet of Edisto Island. Just one week earlier, Maribelle had pleaded with her husband to find a Christmas tree that could be decorated for their daughter, four-year-old Ada. After searching the woods behind his house for hours, Mr. Seymour finally found the perfect tree. It was the prettiest Virginia Pine he'd ever seen. The right size, the tree was full, with strong branches, short needles, a rich shade of green, and the smell of

Christmas. His wife was so excited that she couldn't wait to begin decorating the tree for their only child.

That night, having fed and bathed Ada, the doting mother sat in a rocking chair next to the fireplace and hummed a lullaby. Certain the girl had fallen asleep, Maribelle placed her in her bed just off from the main area of the house. The couple began busying themselves decorating the house and wrapping presents. Having trimmed the tree, the couple was thoroughly exhausted, and ready for bed. The night had grown cold and late. In the fireplace, a small flame hovered above some smoldering coals. Seymour thought it was the right time to enjoy some of the wine in the pretty bottle he'd bought a few days earlier. There had been a big mix-up at the counter with a dissatisfied customer who wanted to return a special bottle of wine. The angry customer went on and on complaining about his purchase to the store owner, demanding that he be allowed to exchange the wine for another bottle, claiming that his wife was extremely unhappy with it. Seymour did not understand what all of the confusion was about. The attractive bottle was clearly still sealed and unopened. It was extremely ornate, wrapped in gold-leaf with shiny crystals on the label that simply read: *"home-made"*. The store owner finally gave in and stepped away from the counter to retrieve a different bottle for the irate customer. In that moment, Seymour, having grown impatient waiting for the store owner to return, pulled out a twenty dollar bill and placed it on the counter, instructing the customer to tell the store owner to keep the change. He picked up the special bottle of wine and left the store, thinking Maribelle would appreciate the beautiful bottle.

As Maribelle stirred coals in the fireplace, Seymour poured two generous glasses of wine. They drank and chatted quietly, but their eyes kept going back to the ornate bottle with the dazzling stones. They decided to stay away until the last embers in the fireplace had burned out. The house had gotten so hot that Maribelle opened the big windows to let in some night air. She pulled a chair under the window and sat there for a moment. By now, Seymour and Maribelle were so intoxicated that they barely made it to their bed. Neither remembered to close the windows. Inebriated, the couple soon fell into a deep sleep. Sometime later, they were startled, awakened when a blast of wind blew through the windows, causing the wooden shutters to bang. The wind, cold and howling, finally disturbed the couple enough so that they both sat up on the bed, shaking and shivering. There was something foreboding about the cold air that seemed to fill the little house.

Maribelle and Seymour glanced over at Ada's empty bed and leapt from their bed, shouting her name. They searched all through, in, and around the house, to no avail. The couple's cries for Ada quickly woke their neighbors. For hours, and into most of the following day, the people of Ravenswood tirelessly searched the woods for Ada. Sadly, there was no sight of the little girl. On the second night, as the Brewsters, sleepless, and losing hope of finding their little girl sat with some of their neighbors, they heard the sound of a child's cry. The crying was distant, but everyone believed it was little Ada, lost and crying in the woods.

Filled with hope, everyone leapt to their feet. The men quickly got lanterns while Maribelle and several of the women gathered quilts and the girl's favorite blanket. The thought of her Ada somewhere in those dark, murky swamps in the dead of winter, wearing only a nightgown, made her tremble.

They hurried off into the forest, trying to find which direction the cries came from. As they made their way through the dense woods, the crying became louder and louder, filling the forest with a sound so intense, that it frightened everyone. When the crying suddenly stopped, Ada's favorite blanket fell from Maribelle's hands onto the damp ground. Without a word, the distraught mother picked up the blanket and slowly walked towards a small pond. Seymour, broken, his tired face, washed in tears, followed his wife. There, at the edge of the pond, laid the beautiful ornate, bottle, the empty bottle they had left near the open window. As they stared into the pond, Ada's little face appeared and floated gently on the water. Slowly, her little face sank deeper and deeper, until it vanished into the dark green water. Maribelle, overcame with uncontrollable grief, plunged hysterically into the pond, grabbing madly at the phantom that had appeared and disappeared before their very eyes. She screamed Ada's name over and over again, each time reaching deeper down into the water. When they had finally calmed Maribelle and dragged her away from the pond, they discovered, clutched in her hand, was a piece of Ada's pink nightgown.

No one ever knew for certain just how Maribelle came to find that fragment from her daughter's night gown. The shallow pond was thoroughly searched and dragged, but Ada was never found, only the mysterious wine bottle. After the tragic loss of their little daughter, the Brewster's, heartbroken and destroyed, were never the same. The couple found it difficult to continue living in Ravenswood with such a sad memory and so, began making plans to move away.

As the story goes, folks say that, late one night, nearly a year after little Ada had gone missing, the Brewsters, still grieving, were awakened by the sounds of a crying child. At first, neither one of them mentioned that it was unmistakably Ada's voice. But the tormenting cries became so loud, that it filled the entire house. Unable to live with the haunting memory of their daughter, the couple packed up and left in the middle of the night. They were never seen or heard from again. The following morning, neighbors found their home abandoned. Inside, next to a chair near the window, sat the mysterious bottle of wine, unopened and unsealed.

References

[1] Sciway.net. Edisto Indians-Native Americans in South Carolina.

[2] Leiferman, Henry. *"An Out-Of-The-Way-Isle in South Carolina"*. The New York Times, April 3, 1994, Section 5. p.8.

[3] The Freedmens' Bureau, Records Of The Bureau Of Refugees, Freedmen and Abandoned Lands, 1865-1870. (Freedmensbureau.com/georgia/land); Freedmens' Land Certificates Issued From Edisto Island, South Carolina by Alden, Agt. Of Bureau.

[4] *"Crossing The Dawhoo—The Dawhoo Bridge"*. Edisto, A Sea Island History, August 31, 2010. (http://www.calgriffin.com/Edisto_Big_Bridge/Page_ 2340968.html)

[5] Spencer, Charles. Edisto Island, 1861 to 2006: Ruin, Recovery, And Rebirth. *("The Black Republic of Edisto Island", Chapter 1)*.Published by The History Press, Charleston, South Carolina, 2008.

[6] Henry Bram ET al. To Major General O.O. Howard, (20 or 21 October, 1865). Letters Received, Ser. 15, Washington Hdqrs., RG 105, From *"After Slavery: Educator Resources"*. A Committee of Freedmen on Edisto Island Reveal Their Expectations

ABOUT THE AUTHOR

A native of Edisto Island, South Carolina, Sandhi Smalls Santini is a New York City-based cabaret performer and writer. She received her B.A. in Journalism and Theatre Arts from Howard University, Washington, DC. Subsequent studies were obtained in Human Rights from Columbia University Graduate School of Arts and Sciences, NYC; and The Playwriting Program at Woodie King Jr.'s New Federal Theatre, NYC. She's a member of SAGAFTRA; The League of Professional Theatre Women; The Society for the Preservation of Theatrical History; and the Edisto Chamber of Commerce. The author of *Poetry and Prose On A Platter,* Sandhi is a features writer for *Routes Magazine: A Guide To African American Culture.*

CPSIA information can be obtained
at www.ICGtesting.com
Printed in the USA
LVHW010057010921
696580LV00017B/2002